Luis Sepúlveda was born in Ovalle, northern Chile, in 1949. Imprisoned by the Pinochet dictatorship, he was for many years a political exile. He has written award-winning novels, short stories, plays and essays, and is one of the world's most widely read Latin American writers. Luis Sepúlveda now lives in Europe, but travel remains his ruling passion.

D0172054

FULL CIRCLE

A South American Journey

Luis Sepúlveda

Translated by Chris Andrews

LONELY PLANET PUBLICATIONS
Melbourne • Oakland • London • Paris

Full Circle: A South American Journey

Published by Lonely Planet Publications
    Head Office: PO Box 617, Hawthorn, Vic 3122, Australia
    Branches: 155 Filbert St, Suite 251, Oakland, CA 94607, USA
                     10 Barley Mow Passage, Chiswick, London W4 4PH, UK
                     71 bis rue du Cardinal Lemoine, 75005 Paris, France

First published in Spain as *Patagonia Express* (Tusquets Editores, Barcelona, 1995)

Published by Lonely Planet Publications, 1996

Printed by SNP Pte Ltd, Singapore

Author photograph by Daniel Mordzinski
Maps by Andrew Tudor

This project has been assisted by the Commonwealth
Government through the Australia Council, its arts
funding and advisory body.

National Library of Australia Cataloguing in Publication Data

Sepúlveda, Luis, 1949-
[Patagonia express. English]
Full Circle: a South American journey.

ISBN 0 86442 465 5.

1. Sepúlveda, Luis, 1949- – Journeys – South America.
2. South America – Description and travel. I. Title.
II. Title: Patagonia express. English.
(Series: Lonely Planet Journeys.)
918

Text © Luis Sepúlveda 1995
By arrangement with Dr Ray-Güde Mertin, Literarische Agentur, Bad Homburg,
Germany.
English-language translation © Lonely Planet 1996
Maps © Lonely Planet 1996

Contents

Part One – Notes from a Journey to Nowhere   9

Part Two – Notes from an Outward Journey   35

Part Three – Notes from a Return Journey   81

Final Part – Note on Arrival   169

Notes on these Notes   185

Glossary   191

Part One

Notes from a Journey to Nowhere

Chapter One

THE TICKET to nowhere was a gift from my grandfather. My grandfather. An extraordinary and terrifying being. I think I had just turned eleven when he gave me the ticket.

We were walking through Santiago one summer morning. The old man had already offered me six or so fizzy drinks, and as many ice creams, which had all well and truly liquefied in my belly. I knew he was waiting to be informed of my need to urinate. Perhaps he really was concerned about my kidneys when he asked:

"What? You don't want a pee, son? Shit! After all you've had to drink . . ."

Under normal circumstances, my reply would have been dramatically affirmative, accompanied by a squeezing

11

together of the legs. Then, removing the butt of the cheap cigar that was always hanging from his lips, he would have sighed before exclaiming in his most didactic tone of voice:

"Hold on, son. Just hold on until we find the right church."

But that morning I was determined to wet my pants if I had to rather than be abused by yet another priest. The joke of filling me up with ice creams and fizzy drinks and then making me urinate on church doors was one we had been repeating ever since I learnt to walk and the old guy adopted me as his fellow freedom-fighter, making me a pint-sized accomplice to the pranks of a retired anarchist.

God knows how many church doors I must have peed on, how many priests and pious women had insulted me.

"You little swine! Don't you have a toilet at home?!" was the gentlest reprimand I heard.

"How dare you insult my grandson! He's a free man! Parasite! Scum! Murderer of social conscience!" While my grandfather harangued them I would let the last drops fall, swearing to myself that next Sunday I wouldn't accept a single Papaya, Bilz or Orange Crush, the drinks he offered me more than generously.

That morning I stood up to the old man.

"Yes. I'm nearly wetting myself, Grandpa. But I want to go to a toilet."

The old guy chewed on the butt of his cigar before spitting it out. Then he murmured, "Bloody hell," and walked a couple of steps away, but came back immediately to ruffle my hair.

"Is it because of last Sunday?" he asked, taking another cigar from his pocket.

"Of course, Grandpa. That priest wanted to kill you."

"Well, those bastards are dangerous, son. Still, if that's the way it is, we'll move on to more significant action."

The previous Sunday I had relieved my bladder onto the hundred-year-old door of the church of San Marcos. It wasn't the first time I had used those ancient planks as a urinal, but the priest must have been on the lookout because he surprised me right in the middle, when it was impossible to stop the stream, and grabbing me by the arm, made me turn around to face my grandfather. Then, pointing at my dripping dick with a prophetic finger, he bellowed:

"It's obvious he's your grandson! You can tell he comes from mean stock!"

What a Sunday. I finished peeing on the steps of the church, terrified by the sight of my grandfather taking off his coat, rolling up his sleeves and challenging the priest to a fist fight – which was only averted by the altar boys and the members of the choir, because the priest accepted the challenge, hitching up his cassock. What a Sunday.

Once I had relieved myself respectably in the toilet of a bar, the old man decided that the best way to finish the morning would be to go to the Asturian Club, where on Sundays the specialities were *fabadas*, made like in the old country, and *cabrales*, the solace of republicans in exile.

To me, *cabrales* was a revolting, foul-smelling lump, eaten only by those old codgers with berets who came round to my grandparents' house each day, always announcing themselves with the same question:

"Don't tell me the old bugger's dead?"

While doing justice to a rice pudding, I wondered what the old man had meant by 'more significant action', and I guess I must have feared the worst, reading a scatological intention into his words. I was reassured when I saw him get up and go with some of the others into the big hall decorated with the red and black flag of the Confederación Nacional del Trabajo. From that hall came the books by Jules Verne, Emilio Salgari, Stevenson and Fenimore Cooper that my grandmother read to me in the afternoons.

I saw him come out with a small book. He called me over, and while I listened to him, I read on the spine of the book: *How the Steel was Tempered*. Nikolay Ostrovsky.

"Now, son, you'll have to read this one by yourself. But before I give it to you, I want you to make two promises."

"Whatever you say, Grandpa."

"This book is an invitation to go on a long journey. Promise me you'll go."

"I promise. But where will I go to, Grandpa?"

"Maybe nowhere, but I assure you it'll be worth it."

"And the second promise?"

"That one day you'll go to Martos."

"Martos? Where is Martos?"

"Here," he said, striking his chest with his hand.

Chapter Two

'THE PATH has two ends, and at both someone is waiting for me', run the words of a well-known Chilean song. The worst of it is that the path does not follow a straight line, but is full of bends, meanders, potholes and detours that always end up taking you nowhere.

How the Steel was Tempered, which I read slowly, asking lots of questions, was responsible for taking me for the first time into that region where dreams are all about nowhere. Like all the youngsters who read Ostrovsky's book, I too wanted to be Pavel Korchaguin, the comrade from Komsomol, the long-suffering protagonist, who is willing to sacrifice everything, even his life, in order to do his duty as a young proletarian. I dreamed of being Pavel Korchaguin, and to make that dream a reality I became a member of the Young Communists.

My grandfather grudgingly accepted the loss of his grandson on Sundays, and for several months was furious with the Spanish translator of *How the Steel was Tempered*. Apparently, the book was supposed to guide me towards libertarian ideas as a first step on the journey to nowhere. But his annoyance lasted only until the day I announced that the students had gone on strike in solidarity with the coal-miners. I only ever saw him drink to excess once, and that was on the day of the strike. Half-pissed, he held back his tears while murmuring:

"My grandson is on strike – a chip off the bloody block."

My grandfather. I remember the first time I made him read a copy of *Youth*, the Young Communists' magazine. He read the four pages carefully and concluded that although it was published by a bunch of Stalinist toadies, it wasn't such a bad way to start understanding the order of things:

"And I don't mean the order the state imposes, that balls-up, but natural order, which results from brotherhood among men."

My parents were thrilled when I became a Young Communist, because a Young Communist had to be top of the class, best in sport, the most cultivated and well mannered of his peers, and at home, a paragon of responsibility and diligence. Within each Young Communist was nurtured the seed of the collective social being who would characterise the new society. So it was that I became a kind of red monk, ascetic and boring. A right pain, as I was told years later by a girl who had refused to be my girlfriend, when, baffled, I asked her why.

Having been a Young Communist for more than six years was like having a permanently valid ticket to nowhere. All my childhood friends had traced out their paths: some were going to study in the United States or Uruguay or Europe, others were going to get a job. But all I wanted to do was to stand firm at my post.

I was eighteen years old when I tried to follow the example of the most universally significant man to have come out of Latin America, Che Guevara. That's when the time came to pay a supplement on the ticket to nowhere.

Chapter Three

UNTIL NOW, I have avoided the theme of prison during the dictatorship in Chile. This is partly because I have always found life fascinating and worth living up to the last breath, and I didn't want to insult it by mentioning such an obscene accident. It is also partly because so many testimonies have been written, unfortunately most of them bad.

I spent two and a half years of my youth locked up in one of the most miserable Chilean jails, in Temuco.

The worst of it wasn't the fact of being locked up, because life went on inside, and was sometimes more interesting than outside. The most highly qualified 'prisoners of war' – and the teaching staffs of all the southern universities were there – set up various faculties, so a lot of us learnt languages, maths, quantum physics, world history, art history or the history of philosophy. Over two weeks, a professor called Iriarte gave a magnificent seminar on Keynes and the political reasoning of contemporary economists, which was attended by several army officers in addition to the hundred or so prisoners. The journalist and writer Andrés Müller discoursed on the tactical errors of the Paris Communards, to the astonishment of the troops guarding the shoemaking workshop, which we had christened the Great Hall of the Temuco Athenaeum. Another famous POW, Genaro Avendaño – he was 'disappeared' in 1979 – moved both prisoners and soldiers with a dramatisation of the writer Unamuno's 1936 Salamanca speech denouncing Franco's Falangists.

We even managed to run a little library which included titles that were absolutely forbidden outside, thanks to the curious censorship practised by the non-commissioned officer in charge of filtering the books sent to us by friends and relatives. We were eternally grateful to him for choosing First Aid as the category in which to classify the pride of our library, a copy of *Open Veins of Latin America*. We even had classes in *haute cuisine*. I will never forget the passion with which Julio Garcés, ex-chef at the Union Club, mecca of the Chilean aristocracy, defended the unmatchable subtlety of rabbit fat, essential to the preparation of a good rabbit-liver sauce, and insisted that it was imperative to cook eel broth with the same white wine that would accompany it on the table. Years later I met Garcés in Belgium. He was the chef at a prestigious restaurant in Brussels, and proudly showed me the two diplomas he had been awarded by the Michelin Guides for his culinary expertise. These elegant documents flanked and set off a third, written by hand on a page from a notebook: the Temuco Michelin, which we had bestowed on him for a marvellous soufflé of seaside memories, made with love, a can of mussels, leftover bread and fragrant leaves from a pot plant which we had to watch like hawks to prevent the prison cats from eating it.

Nine hundred and forty-two days was the duration of my time in that place which belonged to everyone and no-one. Being inside was not the worst thing that could happen to us. It was one more way of resisting. The worst was when they took us to Tucapel for interrogation, roughly once a fortnight. Then we understood that at last we were approaching nowhere.

Chapter Four

THE MILITARY had rather inflated ideas of our destructive capacity. They questioned us about plans to assassinate all the officers in American military history, to blow up bridges and seal off tunnels, and to prepare for the landing of a terrible foreign enemy whom they could not identify.

Temuco is a sad, grey, rainy city. No-one would call it a tourist attraction, and yet the barracks of the Tucapel regiment came to house a sort of permanent international convention of sadists. The Chileans, who were the hosts, after all, were assisted in the interrogations by primates from Brazilian military intelligence – they were the worst – North Americans from the State Department, Argentinian paramilitary personnel, Italian neo-fascists and even some agents of Mossad.

I remember Rudi Weismann, a Chilean with a passion for the South and sailing, who was tortured and interrogated in the gentle language of the synagogues. This infamy was too much for Rudi, who had thrown in his lot with Israel: he had worked on a kibbutz, but in the end his nostalgia for Tierra del Fuego had brought him back to Chile. He simply could not understand how Israel could support such a gang of criminals, and though till then he had always been a model of good humour, he dried up like a neglected plant. One morning we found him dead in his sleeping bag. No need for an autopsy, his face made it clear: Rudi Weismann had died of sadness.

The commander of the Tucapel regiment – a basic respect for paper prevents me from writing his name – was a fanatical admirer of Field Marshal Rommel. When he found a prisoner he liked, he would invite him to recover from the interrogations in his office. After assuring the prisoner that everything that happened in the barracks was in the best interests of our great nation, the commander would offer him a glass of Korn – somebody used to send him this insipid, wheat-based liquor from Germany – and make him sit through a lecture on the Afrika Korps. The guy's parents or grandparents were German, but he couldn't have looked more Chilean: chubby, short-legged, dark untidy hair. You could have mistaken him for a truck

23

driver or a fruit vendor, but when he talked about Rommel he became the caricature of a Nazi guard.

At the end of the lecture he would dramatise Rommel's suicide, clicking his heels, raising his right hand to his forehead to salute an invisible flag, muttering "Adieu geliebtes Vaterland," and pretending to shoot himself in the mouth. We all hoped that one day he would do it for real.

There was another curious officer in the regiment: a lieutenant struggling to contain a homosexuality that kept popping out all over the place. The soldiers had nicknamed him Daisy, and he knew it.

We could all tell that it was a torment for Daisy not to be able to adorn his body with truly beautiful objects, and the poor guy had to make do with the regulation paraphernalia. He wore a .45 pistol, two cartridge clips, a commando's curved dagger, two hand grenades, a torch, a walkie-talkie, the insignia of his rank and the silver wings of the parachute corps. The prisoners and the soldiers thought he looked like a Christmas tree.

This individual sometimes surprised us with generous and apparently disinterested acts – we didn't know that the Stockholm syndrome could be a military perversion. For example, after the interrogations he would suddenly fill our pockets with cigarettes or the highly prized aspirin tablets with vitamin C. One afternoon he invited me to his room.

"So you're a man of letters," he said, offering me a can of Coca-Cola.

"I've written a couple of stories. That's all," I replied.

"You're not here for an interrogation. I'm very sorry about what's happening, but that's what war is like. I want us to talk as one writer to another. Are you surprised? The army has produced some great men of letters. Think of Don Alonso de Ercilla y Zúñiga, for example."

"Or Cervantes," I added.

Daisy included himself among the greats. That was his problem. If he wanted adulation, he could have it. I drank the Coca-Cola and thought about Garcés, or rather, about his chicken, because, incredible as it seems, the cook had a chicken called Dulcinea, the name of Don Quixote's mistress.

One morning it jumped the wall which separated the common-law prisoners from the POWs, and it must have been a chicken with deep political convictions, because it decided to stay with us. Garcés caressed it and sighed, saying: "If I had a pinch of pepper and a pinch of cumin, I'd make you a chicken marinade like you've never tasted."

"I want you to read my poems and give me your opinion, your honest opinion," said Daisy, handing me a notebook.

I left that room with my pockets full of cigarettes, caramel sweets, tea bags and a tin of US Army marmalade.

That afternoon I started to believe in the brotherhood of writers.

They transported us from the prison to the barracks and back in a cattle truck. The soldiers made sure there was plenty of cow shit on the floor of the truck before ordering us to lie face down with our hands behind our necks. We were guarded by four of them, with North American machine guns, one in each corner of the truck. They were almost all young guys brought down from northern garrisons, and the harsh climate of the South kept them flu-ridden and in a perpetually filthy mood. They had orders to fire on the bundles – us – at the slightest suspect movement, or on any civilian who tried to approach the truck. But as time wore on, the discipline gradually relaxed and they turned a blind eye to the packet of cigarettes or piece of fruit thrown from a window, or the pretty and daring girl who ran beside the truck blowing us kisses and shouting: "Don't give up, comrades! We'll win!"

Back in prison, as always, we were met by the welcoming committee organised by Doctor 'Skinny' Pragnan, now an eminent psychiatrist in Belgium. First he examined those who couldn't walk and those who had heart problems, then those who had come back with a dislocation or with ribs out of place. Pragnan was expert at estimating how much electricity had been put into us on the grill, and patiently determined who would be able to absorb liquids in the next few hours. Then finally it was time to take communion: we were given the aspirin with vitamin C and an anticoagulant to prevent internal haematomas.

"Dulcinea's days are numbered," I said to Garcés, and looked for a corner in which to read Daisy's notebook.

The elegantly inscribed pages were redolent of love, honey, sublime suffering and forgotten flowers. By the third page I knew that Daisy hadn't even gone to the trouble of reusing the ideas of the Mexican poet Amado Nervo – he'd simply copied out his poems word for word.

I called out to Peyuco Gálvez, a Spanish teacher, and read him a couple of lines.

"What do you think, Peyuco?"

"Amado Nervo. The book is called *The Interior Gardens*."

I had got myself into a real jam. If Daisy found out that I knew the work of this sugary poet Nervo, then it wasn't Garcés's chicken whose days were numbered, but mine. It was a serious problem, so that night I presented it to the Council of Elders.

"Now, Daisy, would he be the passive or the active type?" enquired Iriarte.

"Stop it, will you. My skin's at risk here," I replied.

"I'm serious. Maybe our friend wants to have an affair

with you, and giving you the notebook was like dropping a silk handkerchief. And like a fool you picked it up. Perhaps he copied out the poems for you to find a message in them. I've known queens who seduced boys by lending them *Demian* by Hermann Hesse. If Daisy is the passive type, this business with Amado Nervo means he wants to test your nerve, so to speak. And if he's the active type, well, it would have to hurt less than a kick in the balls."

"Message my arse. He gave you the poems as his own, and you should say you liked them a lot. If he was trying to send a message, he should have given the notebook to Garcés; he's the only one who has an interior garden. Or maybe Daisy doesn't know about the pot plant," remarked Andrés Müller.

"Let's be serious about this. You have to say something to him, and Daisy mustn't even suspect that you know Nervo's poems," declared Pragnan.

"Tell him you liked the poems, but that the adjectives strike you as a bit excessive. Quote Huidobro: when an adjective doesn't give life, it kills. That way you'll show him that you read his poems carefully and that you are criticising his work as a colleague," suggested Gálvez.

The Council of Elders approved of Gálvez's idea, but I spent two weeks on tenterhooks. I couldn't sleep. I wished they would come and take me to be kicked and electrocuted so I could give the damned notebook back. In those two weeks I came to hate good old Garcés:

"Listen, mate, if everything goes well, and you get a little jar of capers as well as the cumin and the pepper, we'll have such a feast with that chicken."

After a fortnight, I found myself at last stretched out face down on the mattress of cowpats with my hands behind my neck. I thought I was going mad: I was happy to be heading towards a session of the activity known as torture.

Tucapel barracks. Service Corps. In the background, the perpetual green of Cerro Ñielol, sacred to the Mapuche Indians. There was a waiting room outside the interrogation cell, like at the doctor's. There they made us sit on a bench with our hands tied behind our backs and black hoods over our heads. I never understood what the hoods were for, because once we got inside they took them off, and we could see the interrogators – the toy soldiers who, with panic-stricken faces, turned the handle of the generator, and the health officers who attached the electrodes to our anuses, testicles, gums and tongue, and then listened with stethoscopes to see who was faking and who had really passed out on the grill.

Lagos, a deacon of the Emmaus International ragmen, was the first to be interrogated that day. For a year they had been working him over to find out how the organisation had come by a couple of dozen old military uniforms which had been found in their warehouses. A trader who sold army surplus gear had donated them. Lagos screamed in pain and repeated over and over what the soldiers wanted to hear: the uniforms belonged to an invading army which was preparing to land on the Chilean coast.

I was waiting for my turn when someone took off the hood. It was Lieutenant Daisy.

"Follow me," he ordered.

We went into an office. On the desk I saw a tin of cocoa and a carton of cigarettes which were obviously there to reward my comments on his literary work.

"Did you read my poesy?" he asked, offering me a seat.

Poesy. Daisy said poesy, not poetry. A man covered with pistols and grenades can't say 'poesy' without sounding ridiculous and effete. At that moment he revolted me, and I decided that even if it meant pissing blood, hissing when I spoke and being able to charge batteries just by touching them, I wasn't going to lower myself to flattering a plagiarising faggot in uniform.

"You have pretty handwriting, Lieutenant. But you know these poems aren't yours," I said, giving him back the notebook.

I saw him begin to shake. He was carrying enough arms to kill me several times over, and if he didn't want to stain

30

his uniform, he could order someone else to do it. Trembling with anger he stood up, threw what was on the desk onto the floor and shouted:

"Three weeks in the cube. But first, you're going to visit the chiropodist, you piece of subversive shit!"

The chiropodist was a civilian, a landholder who had lost several thousand hectares in the land reform, and who was getting his revenge by participating in the interrogations as a volunteer. His speciality was peeling back toenails, which led to terrible infections.

I knew the cube. I had spent my first six months of prison there in solitary confinement: it was an underground cell, one and a half metres wide by one and a half metres long by one and a half metres high. In the old days there had been a tannery in the Temuco jail, and the cube was used to store fat. The walls still stank of fat, but after a week your excrement fixed that, making the cube very much a place of your own.

You could only stretch out across the diagonal, but the low temperatures of southern Chile, the rainwater and the soldiers' urine made you want to curl up hugging your legs and stay like that, wishing yourself smaller and smaller, so that eventually you could live on one of the islands of floating shit, which conjured up images of dream holidays. I was there for three weeks, running through Laurel and

Hardy films, remembering the books of Salgari, Stevenson and London word by word, playing long games of chess, licking my toes to protect them from infection. In the cube I swore over and over again never to become a literary critic.

Chapter Five

ONE DAY in June 1976, the journey to nowhere came to an end. Thanks to the activities of Amnesty International I was released from jail, and with my head shaved and twenty kilos lighter, I filled my lungs with the rich air of a freedom limited by the fear of losing it again. Many of those who stayed inside were killed by the military. It makes me proud to know that I have neither forgotten nor forgiven their executioners. Many things in my life have given me great satisfaction, but nothing compares with the happiness that comes from opening a bottle of wine on learning that one of those criminals has been gunned down in the street. On such occasions, I raise my glass and say: "One son of a bitch less. Here's to life!"

In my travels I have met with some of those who

survived; others I have not seen again, but each has a place of honour in my memory.

One day, near the end of 1985, I ran into Gálvez in a bar in Valencia. He told me he was living in Milan, where he had become an Italian citizen, and had four beautiful daughters, all of them Italian. After a long, tearful hug, we got talking about old times, and naturally the chicken came up.

"May it rest in peace," said Gálvez. "I was the last of the old lot to be released, at the end of '78, and I took it with me. It lived out its days fat and happy at my house in Los Angeles. It's buried in the garden under a stone which reads: 'Here lies Dulcinea, mistress of preposterous knights, empress of nowhere'."

Part Two

Notes from an Outward Journey

Chapter One

I KNEW the border wasn't far away. Another border, but I couldn't see it. The only thing that stood out in the monotonous Andean evening was the sun's reflection off a metal structure. That was where La Quiaca and Argentina finished. On the other side was Villazón, in Bolivian territory.

In a little over two months I had followed the roads that lead from Santiago de Chile to Buenos Aires, from Montevideo to Pelotas, and from São Paulo to Santos, where my chances of embarking on a boat bound for Africa or Europe went down the drain.

In the airport at Santiago, the soldiers had stamped my passport with an enigmatic letter 'F'. Felon? Fool? Free? Freak? I don't know if there is a language in which the word 'leper' begins with 'F', but I do know that my passport made people recoil whenever I opened it in the office of a shipping company.

"No. We don't want Chileans who have passports stamped 'F'."

"Can you tell me what the hell the 'F' means?"

"Come on, you know just as well as I do. Good afternoon."

Looking on the bright side, I had time, all the time in the world, so I decided to get on a boat in Panama. From Santos to the Canal is about four thousand kilometres, just a stroll for someone with a taste for the road.

Riding on clapped-out buses, trucks and lethargic trains, I made it to Asunción, the city of transparent sadness, perpetually swept by a desolate wind blowing from the Chaco. From Paraguay, I went back to Argentina and, after crossing the little-known region of Humahuaca, arrived in La Quiaca with the intention of going on to La Paz. Then . . . well, all in good time. The important thing was to ride out the days of fear as boats at sea ride out coastal storms.

I felt as if the omnipresent fear of that time was hounding me.

In every town where I stayed, I visited old acquaintances or began to make new friends. With just a few exceptions, these encounters left me with the same bitter taste: people were living in and for fear. They had turned it into a labyrinth without an exit. Fear sat in on their conversations and meals. They performed even the most trivial acts with a shameless prudence, and at night they didn't go to bed in order to dream of better days or days gone by, but to hurl themselves into a swamp of thick, dark fear, a fear that occupied the dead hours and got them out of bed in the morning bag-eyed and even more afraid.

I spent one night of the journey in São Paulo trying, hopelessly, to make love. It was a failure, redeemed only by the woman's feet calling to my own in the honest language of skin and daybreak.

"Well, we made a mess of that," I think I remarked.

"Sure did. As if we were being watched. As if we were using bodies and time borrowed from fear," she replied.

Feet. Those ineffectual, squat little creatures caressed each other while we shared a cigarette.

"Once it was so easy to get to the country of happiness. It wasn't on any map, but everyone knew how to get there. There were unicorns and forests of marijuana. Now we've lost the border," she added.

I arrived in La Quiaca in the evening, and as soon as I got off the train I felt the buffeting cold of the Andes. I was going to open my pack and get out a jumper, but changed my mind and decided instead to walk quickly to somewhere warm. I ended up jogging to a ticket office.

"I want to go to La Paz tomorrow. Can you tell me what time the train leaves?"

The ticket vendor was brewing maté. He was holding a big gourd with a silver base. The herb smelt good: it was giving off that aroma happily poised between bitter and sweet. I thought how well a maté would go down in that cold.

The ticket vendor looked at me, scrutinised my face from ear to ear, from forehead to chin, then looked away. It was fear; he was consulting the poster with the photographs of wanted men. He didn't offer me a maté, and before replying, he put the gourd aside.

"You'll have to ask the Bolivians. The border is a stone's throw away, but they're not there now." The ticket vendor had a lilting accent; he sounded as if he came from Salta or La Rioja.

Next to the station was a dreary hotel, like all hotels in unimportant towns. When I got to my room – a bronze bedstead, a wobbly bedside table, a candlestick with a short stub of candle, a jar of water and a stiff cloth trying to pass itself off as a towel – I opened my pack and put on a thick jumper. It was as cold in the room as outside, but the bed would be alright for one night. The sheets were excessively starched and had the same wooden stiffness as the towel, but the blankets were thick and made of real wool. I remembered that someone – who could it have been? – maintained that the cold was the best ally of hotel hygiene.

I left the hotel to look around La Quiaca, and started walking through the silent, empty streets between mud houses that blended into the nearby mountains as the shadows lengthened. After a few blocks I saw a place that was open. It smelt of grilled meat and, prompted by my growling stomach, I went in and sat down at a table covered with wrapping paper.

"We only have grilled ribs," said the waiter. He was a squat little man with broad shoulders and short legs; a shock of hair, stiff as a brush, framed his totemic face. He hissed when he said a word with *s* in it, as if his teeth were stuck together.

The meat was delicious. The fat it exuded as the knife sank in was a pleasure to soak up with bread. The wine was a bit sour, but it gladdened the body.

When I had finished eating, I ordered a glass of *caña*, and abandoned myself to a well-earned burp. Then I saw the old man.

He was wearing an old brown leather jacket. He came in and put a pair of work gloves and a metal lantern on the table.

He nodded in reply to the waiter's gestures, and as soon as the jug of wine arrived, took a long draught with closed eyes and the satisfaction of someone who has just finished a long day's work. I went up to him.

"Excuse me, sir. Are you a railway official?"

"Yes and no," he answered.

His reply surprised me and made me uneasy, but then I saw that he was offering me a seat.

"Yes, I work for the railways; but no, I'm not an official, I'm a labourer."

"I see. Excuse me."

"Chilean, are you?"

"So it seems."

"Do you want something to eat?"

I thanked him, explaining that I had already eaten, and asked him about the timetable for the trains to La Paz. At this point the meat arrived. The old man's eyes gleamed and he wiped his knife and fork with the serviette.

"Enjoy your meal."

"Thanks. You want some wine?"

Without waiting for my reply, he clicked his fingers to order another glass. He put the first piece of meat into his mouth and a dreamy look came into his eyes.

"It's the best beef there is: grilled ribs. What a noble creature the cow is – steaks all over the place, but the ribs are the best."

"That's what I think, too. Cheers."

"Cheers. You know what they need up here in the North? *Chimichurri*. That's what they need. Grilled meat without *chimichurri* is like verse without rhyme."

"Couldn't agree more."

The old man chewed with macrobiotic care. A few drops of juice tried to escape from the corners of his mouth, but the rapidity of his tongue was implacable. When he had chewed sufficiently, he washed the mouthfuls down with abundant wine.

"So you're going to La Paz. Watch out for mountain sickness up there. If you feel it coming on, eat onion. Get some onion into your system. La Paz, you say. The train leaves between eight and midday; it's not very punctual, to put it mildly. Have you got a ticket?"

He spoke without looking at me. All his attention was fixed on the piece of meat as it disappeared in a delicate agony of juices, finally leaving the plate clean.

"No. I haven't bought it yet," I said. I had half a mind to go, but the old man ordered another jug of wine.

"Excuse my bad manners, but I was just so hungry. I'd been more than twelve hours without a bite, you know."

"It's OK."

"You don't have a ticket then. Well, you'd better cross the border early. The soldiers open it at seven and there's always a queue."

"I'll try to be near the start of it."

"Good, but that won't be enough. At the ticket counter the Bolivians will tell you there's no room left, that all the tickets have been sold. That's what they'll tell you. The bastards. And you know what you have to do then? Fold up a bill, a fifty, know what I mean?"

"I see. Thanks for the tip."

The old man started looking at me mischievously. He took a long silver pin from the lapel of his jacket and picked his teeth with it.

"So, you're a Chilean then."

"Well, you have to be born somewhere."

"Things aren't going too well over there either, are they?"

'Things.' If there was one thing I hated, it was rhetorical questions, and in those days of fear, talking about such 'things' was not particularly wise.

"Like everywhere, I guess."

"You're right. The world is rotten."

Nor was it a good idea to have a philosophical discussion about universal rottenness with a stranger. I started to get up, but the old man slapped me on the arm.

"You know what, my Chilean friend?"

"No. What?"

"I'm still hungry. That's what. What about we order another serve of the ribs, and you take care of half of it."

I thought about those wretched days of fear, and the journey during which I had normally eaten alone and in a hurry, and it struck me that staying put at this table for a couple of hours was a form of resistance.

"Alright, but the wine's on me."

"Great!" exclaimed the old man, holding out his hand.

We ate. We drank. We talked about a kid with promise, a certain Maradona, very similar to Chamaco Valdés in his mastery of the ball; we compared the punches of Oscar Ringo Bonavena to those of Martín Vargas; we agreed that the emotional intensity of Carlitos couldn't be matched, but that when it came to comparing voices, Julio Sosa, the master of the tango, was in a league of his own. It was like a family occasion at that table covered with wrapping paper, an ordinary evening in Latin America, shared by an Argentinian and a Chilean. Fear stayed outside; an invisible, intractable doorman judged it undesirable and turned it away.

At the end of the meal, the old man reminded me of the need to arrive early at the border, and made a fist of his left hand with the thumb extended to indicate a point that might have been falling from the sky or somewhere behind his back.

"It's very close. The other side begins with the train," he said.

45

In the hotel the bed was very cold, possibly damp, and it took me a fair while to warm up. I was weary from the journey and the five glasses of wine I had downed with the railwayman. I wanted to sleep, but I was afraid of missing the train. The idea of spending another day in La Quiaca didn't appeal to me. Luckily I had plenty of cigarettes; they shortened the night.

Dawn arrived without warning, as if a great hand had violently ripped the curtain of darkness, and torrents of eye-injuring light came in through the window. I looked at the clock; it was six in the morning. A good time to walk to the border.

Soon I came to the strange construction I had seen the day before: an iron bridge. At one end, an armoured enclosure painted in the colours of the Argentinian flag. At the other end, another casemate, in the colours of the Bolivian flag. There was no river flowing under the bridge.

At seven o'clock exactly, Argentinian soldiers, still half-asleep, opened the border post. There were lots of people: women, men and children with enigmatic faces, who spoke among themselves in their sibilant Aymara, lumps of chewed coca leaves swelling their cheeks. They were carrying suitcases, parcels, bundles of herbs, fruit and vegetables, chickens hanging by their feet – white-eyed, with wings clumsily stretched out – kitchen utensils and indefinable artefacts. At the other end of the bridge a similar group was waiting, and I remembered the railwayman's words when I saw that the train tracks began beside the Bolivian casemate.

The Argentinian border guards checked my passport, compared the photo with those on the poster of wanted men, and gave it back to me without a word. I crossed the bridge. Goodbye Argentina. Hello Bolivia.

The Bolivians repeated the ceremony, but this time with a soldier asking questions.

"Where are you going to?"

"La Paz."

"Do you have a ticket?"

"No. That's why I've come early."

"How many days are you going to spend in Bolivia? Do you have a place to stay in La Paz?"

"No. I'm going to keep travelling."

"Where to?"

Where to? I hesitated. I thought of the little school map of South America in my pack. It was a map full of evocative names, and I could have said Lima, Guayaquil, Bogotá, Cartagena, Paramaribo or Belém, but the only name that came out was one I had heard my grandfather speak.

"To Martos . . . in Spain."

The soldier let me go through, but I felt the hatred in his

47

stare. He had the eyes of an angry god. Eyes of black fire in a face of stone.

At the Villazón station I followed the railwayman's instructions, and the carefully folded fifty-peso bill transformed the ticket vendor's refusal into a complaint about those who turn up at the last minute to buy their tickets. The station was smaller than the one in La Quiaca. It had two spotlessly clean cement platforms.

"The train arrives between eight and ten, it fills up between ten and twelve, and it leaves when it's full," the ticket vendor told me.

I had time to look around a bit. I bought two *empanadas* and a mug of coffee from a stall. Sitting on my pack, I watched the station become a cheerful market where foodstuffs, fruit, artefacts and farmyard animals were traded. I sat there contentedly, taking in this unfamiliar reality.

At eight, the sun began to beat down hard. Its blinding effect was intensified by the reflection off the whitewashed walls. I was cleaning my sunglasses when I heard a familiar voice, the voice of the railwayman.

"Clear out, Chilean, clear out."

I turned my head around. The old man passed by without looking at me, but murmuring through his teeth:

"Clear out, Chilean, before they get hold of you."

The Andean sun had stopped the clock, the rotation of

the earth and the capricious spinning of the universe. There was not a cloud in the sky, nor a bird, but suddenly, as if they had heard a secret signal, the echo of a trumpet's warning note that had been resounding for centuries among the lonely hills, the totemic beings packed up their wares, and a wordless gust of fear blew over the platforms and swept away the cheerful market.

Looking towards the beginning of the tracks and the border, I saw a squad of soldiers getting out of a truck. In response to the gestures of an officer they fanned out, ready for an ambush. And I was alone, sitting on my pack.

Just at that moment a whistle sounded, making me look in the opposite direction, and I saw the old diesel locomotive pulling into the station. It was a big green animal, with a yellow scar on its belly, and it snorted like an old dragon as it hauled the train. I saw the grey wagons pass like a series of sad fish with the words La Paz repeated on their gills.

The locomotive stopped when it got to the bridge, because, as the railwayman said, the other side begins with the train. Then they pushed me against a wall, and I stayed there with my legs spread wide open and my hands on the whitewash, while gloved hands emptied my pack and trashed books, photographs and memories that had withstood the days of fear, until, hitting me with the butts of their guns, they made me lie face down and put my hands behind my neck.

Two hours passed before the soldiers went hunting again and made another backpacker lie down beside me. He was an Argentinian, a follower of the Hare Krishnas. With the sun shining off his shaved head and his body wrapped in an incongruous orange robe, he kept wishing them eternal peace.

"What is going on, brother?" he asked quietly.

"Shut your mouth, or they'll shut it for you."

"But what have we done wrong, brother?"

"Called people 'brother' when they don't have any, maybe."

The hours went by and the cramps became less painful. But the yearning for a smoke persisted, and from the point of view of a humiliated reptile, I watched the wheels of the train, the agile feet of the passengers, the suitcases and bundles suddenly becoming weightless and ascending. When the whistle blew and the wheels began to move, I felt that my only chance of leaving the days of fear behind was slipping away, and that I would remain their prisoner, perhaps for ever.

"I told them the truth, the whole truth," complained the Hare Krishna.

"So did I. Some people are just suspicious."

"I told them I'm flying from La Paz to Calcutta. I showed them the ticket, my papers and everything."

"Like I said, some people are just suspicious."

"I am searching for the light. This is a test, brother."

"You are."

"The light is in Calcutta."

At five in the afternoon, they let us stand up. Both of us were sunburnt and blistered on the arms and neck. After a quick bit of paperwork they took away our money and our watches, then expelled us from Bolivia as undesirable aliens.

At the other end of the bridge, the old railwayman was waiting for us with a jug of water and a jar of cream for our burnt skin.

"You were lucky, boys. Those animals could have taken you back to the barracks and then it would have been farewell to the pampa. You were lucky."

"I'll get to Calcutta," the Hare Krishna assured us.

I didn't doubt that he would, and as I walked away with the old man, I sincerely hoped he would get there soon, because if that bald backpacker dressed in orange made it to Calcutta, then one at least, out of thousands, would have found the lost border, and crossed over into the territory of happiness.

Chapter Two

IN THE years after 1973, more than a million Chileans left their long, thin, sick land behind them. Some were forced into exile, some were fleeing from the fear of poverty, others simply wanted to try their luck in the North. Those in the last group were all headed for one place: the United States.

Most of them sold their few belongings to buy a bus ticket to Guayaquil or Quito. They thought that from there it was just a hop, skip and a jump to the promised land in the North.

After travelling for several days, they got off the buses stiff, sweaty and hungry, and when they enquired about how to continue the journey, they discovered that South America is enormous, and that, to make things worse, further north the Panamerican Highway vanished, swallowed up by the Colombian jungle. They were left there, in between, like boats adrift, without a present or a future.

One such stranded traveller was the pianist at the Ali Kan brothel, a long, thin individual, white as a candle. His perpetually bloodshot eyes and the two yellow teeth resting on his bottom lip made him look like a sad rabbit.

He couldn't hold back the tears when he remembered Valparaíso, and the days when he played in the band at the American Bar – the hundred-year-old haunt of the port's bohemians, rubbed off the map by the military when they imposed a curfew which ended up lasting for thirteen years.

"Now that was a decent place. The girls weren't whores; they were young ladies. And the sailors left fantastic tips for the musicians, not like in this pigsty," he would complain, before cursing himself for having washed up in Puerto Bolívar (it's definitely the sort of place you wash up in).

Puerto Bolívar is on the Pacific coast, near Machala, south of Guayaquil. You can sense the sea in the breeze, which sometimes succeeds in dissipating the hot, humid breath coming from inland. You can see the ocean and hear it, but you can't smell it.

The bananas of Ecuador are exported from Puerto Bolívar to destinations all over the world. About five kilometres away from the jetty there is a sinkhole as wide as a football stadium and no-one knows how deep. It is the last resting place of all the bananas which are not fit to be exported because they have started to ripen too early or are marked by parasites, or because the plantation owner, or the carrier, forgot to pay one of the taxes demanded by the industry mafia.

The place is called the Pot and it's always boiling. The thousands of tons of constantly rotting fruit form a thick, sickening, bubbling paste. Everything that is no use ends up in the Pot, and this monstrous stew does not just absorb vegetable matter: the enemies of political strongmen rot there too, with several ounces of lead in their bodies, or mutilated by machetes. The Pot never stops boiling. Its stink is so strong that it overpowers the smell of the sea and keeps even the vultures away.

"Get out of here, get out of here right now, before the stink kills your willpower and you end up like me, rotting alive," the pianist told me every time we met.

I went to Machala because I wanted to get out of Ecuador quickly, and the only way to speed up such departures is to not be fussy about the work you take on. So I accepted a contract for a semester at the University of Machala, which committed me to explaining the sociological aspects of the media to a handful of students. I wanted to leave almost as soon as I got there, but I was broke and had to wait till the end of the contract period to get paid. An eminently tropical bureaucratic rule was to blame for the arrangement whereby visiting teachers (they called us professors) were paid after the end of the semester by an administrator who kept half the cash.

In order to save a bit of the money that we didn't have, a group of us – a Uruguayan, an Argentinian, two Chileans, a Canadian and a guy from Quito with a deep-seated hatred of the tropics – decided to live together in one big room painted a scandalous green, with a galvanised-iron roof and views of the jungle. We hung up six hammocks, and in the afternoons we lay in them rocking, smoking, talking about what we would do when they paid us, getting through crates of beer and watching the blades of the fan spin ineffectually over our heads.

In Machala there was little to see and less to do. Taste was not among the outstanding qualities of the priest whose job it was to censor the films shown in the open-air cinema, so for relief from the heat of the night infused with the stink of the Pot, our only options were to visit the casino or the brothels of Puerto Bolívar. We went to the casino to enjoy the air conditioning, and because there was always one or other of our students there losing in a few minutes as much money as we would be paid for sweating through a semester.

"A round of drinks for the profs," the student would call out, his eyes fixed on the roulette ball.

We would thank him and wish him luck.

We enjoyed going to the brothels, especially the Ali Kan – a huge wooden shed with a galvanised-iron roof run by Doña Evarista, a fat Chilean woman around sixty who sweated and whimpered on our shoulders during her attacks of nostalgia for Santiago or Buenos Aires, the cities in which she had made her début in the profession. Asking Doña Evarista for a dance would get you a bottle of whisky and a carton of cigarettes on the house. We all danced the tango reasonably well, except for the Canadian, who was always busy taking notes on everything he saw and heard for a novel which, according to him, was going to be better than *One Hundred Years of Solitude*. The fat lady was desperately in love with the Canadian, and every time she saw him writing she made the girls keep quiet.

About twenty women worked in the Ali Kan, attending to their clients in tiny rooms with mattresses on the floor. The building was raised on stilts, and when some vigorous sailor's amorous excesses made it shake, the guests in the salon gave him a hearty round of applause. That's how we spent our nights. Our nights at the Ali Kan.

The next day the tropical routine began again: waking to the stink of the Pot, jumping out of the hammock, straightening out my spine, emptying cockroaches and scorpions out of my shoes, taking a long shower, going out into the sticky fug of the street, drinking a cup of that great bitter coffee in a bar, walking five blocks, getting to the university and taking another shower before the classes started.

Fifteen students had enrolled in my course on the sociology of the media, but I only ever met three of them, and I always wondered what the hell they came for. At the age of twenty, one was already an expert on venereal diseases; he had had them all and bragged about it. Another, the son of a banana magnate, spent his mornings conscientiously studying brochures for sports cars. He was obsessed by the idea of owning a Porsche. It didn't seem to bother him at all that there were hardly any roads in the area. And the third student, well, I never even found out if he could read.

After three months I began to think that the pianist at the Ali Kan was right. I had to get out of that hole.

The good people of Machala had never looked kindly on us: six men, five of them foreigners, who lived on credit and frequented the brothels. They didn't look kindly on us, but they didn't mess us about either. They accorded us a kind of acceptance, based on repulsion and mistrust, which lasted until the afternoon when one of the girls at the Ali Kan told us, with tears in her eyes, that the priest had

57

stopped her and two of her colleagues from going to the cinema, and they had missed out on seeing *Cat Ballou*.

"Why did it have to be a film with that gorgeous Lee Marvin?" she whimpered.

Down on our luck, but gentlemen still, the six musketeers set out at once to tell the priest a thing or two.

"Women of ill repute are not allowed into the cinema," pronounced the clergyman.

"It's culture. By watching a film, they might find moral values to make them change their ways. After all, you're the one who chooses the films," argued the Argentinian.

"Quite so. But they must be accompanied by persons of moral standing."

"University professors, for example?" asked the Canadian.

"You lot? Come off it, you wouldn't risk your careers by going to the movies with whores!"

From that day on, we went to the cinema with the girls every Friday. Stationed at the door, the priest looked at us with hatred in his eyes, but he couldn't stop our partners going in. We were doing our duty as gentlemen, but the good people of Machala didn't see it that way. The local teachers stopped inviting us round, the police looked at us mockingly, and rumour had it that we were part-time pimps. The time had come to get out of there. The problem was: how? There was still a long while to go before the end of the semester.

My chance to get back on the road came up one night in the casino. I was enjoying the low temperature which had the gamblers sneezing and gave the ladies of Machala an opportunity to show off their furs. My colleagues had gone to the Ali Kan on account of a miracle that had occurred the previous night: the Canadian, having downed half a bottle of rum, had finally decided to ask the fat lady for a dance. Tango, salsa, merengue, creole waltzes, pasillos, sanjuanitos – he danced them all. Spinning like a top, the Canadian declared that his work in progress was a heap of shit, and distributed his sheets of notes to the clients. Hugging Doña Evarista, who was beside herself with joy, he announced that he was going to live instead, intensely, with his great love. The fat lady invited us to an engagement dinner, and I was going, naturally, but first I wanted to feel that wonderful cold that actually made you want to go outside. That's what I was doing when a hand clamped onto my shoulder.

It was a guy I knew by sight. I knew he was in the banana-transport business; he owned trucks and boats. From his slow, melodious speech, I guessed he was from Guayaquil.

"Listen, prof, do you believe in the law of probabilities?"

"There's something in it."

"Look: I've bet on zero six times in a row, and it hasn't come up. Do you reckon it will next time?"

"The only way to find out is to risk it."

"Spoken like a man. That's what I like to hear," he said, and threw a bunch of keys onto the table.

"New-model Chrysler. Cost me twenty thousand dollars."

The croupier excused himself for a moment, went to an adjoining room and came back very smartly.

"Ten thousand, and five per cent commission for the casino."

"Fifteen thousand, and I'll double the commission."

"The casino accepts the stake. Play, gentlemen."

The ball went round and the man from Guayaquil followed its orbit with an impassive gaze. He rested his hands on the edges of the table without showing the slightest sign of emotion. He was a true gambler. It seemed from his weariness that he wanted to lose. When the ball stopped on seven, he shrugged his shoulders.

"Shit. Well, now we know, prof."

"Sorry."

"That's luck. Let's go to the bar. I'll buy you a drink."

At the bar we introduced ourselves. The guy wanted to find out about me, and after listening quietly, he said, as if he were talking to a banana trader:

"You're just the man I'm looking for, prof. You're coming to live with me for a couple of months at Rocafuerte. I've got a son who's just about to finish high school and I want him to be a lawyer. You coach him into university and I'll solve any money problems you might have. Deal?"

"Anyone can get into university in Ecuador."

"My son's going to study in the United States. There they have entrance exams and all that sort of thing. What about two thousand dollars a month? No, let's make a more practical arrangement, prof: here's a blank cheque. Cash it tomorrow. Take out a thousand or two thousand dollars, whatever you need. But I want you in my house by the end of the week. Off you go now, prof. I like to be alone after losing."

I got to the Ali Kan after midnight. Doña Evarista had made dozens of *empanadas*, which tasted better than beluga caviar in that culinary hell, where the staple diet was rice and banana chips. That night we celebrated on a grand scale. Doña Evarista recognised the signature on the cheque as that of one of the richest men in the region, so my problems were over, and I could consider myself mobile again.

We gobbled down the *empanadas*, emptied countless bottles of Chilean wine, and after singing tangos that drew torrents of tears from the fat lady, the Canadian surprised us with a speech which he gave standing on a table:

"Friends, I want to tell you that this is a wonderful woman and that tomorrow I'm going to come and live with her. I'm going to be the man of this house, and you, my friends, my brothers, from now on you will be like sons to us. Long live the sons of whores!"

The next day I went to the bank, took out a considerable amount of money, paid some debts, distributed some cash among my friends, put on my pack and set out for the bus terminal. Waiting for me there I found the pianist, long, thin and white as a candle.

"You don't know how happy it makes me, my boy. Good luck," he said, shaking my hand.

Before getting onto the bus I took a deep breath, filling my lungs with the rotten air exhaled by the Pot, and from the loudspeakers in the square I heard the voice of the priest threatening to excommunicate anyone who went to see the film *Kramer versus Kramer*, condemning it as a vindication of divorce.

"This afternoon the cinema will be full," murmured the pianist.

Several years later, and a long way from Ecuador, I recognized the name of the Canadian from Machala in a Quebec literary journal. He had published a short story entitled 'All Cats are Grey in the Tropics'. It was a fine piece of writing, and it referred to a certain period spent living with five individuals in a country permeated by the stench of hell. It was a good story, and those were good times, spent waiting for a salary that was never paid, under the blades of a fan that hardly stirred the air, but in the company of fine women and men who offered me the best of themselves.

Chapter Three

THAT MORNING I got up before dawn, packed up my few belongings and said goodbye to the La Conquistada estate. It was a pretty place, a splendid green oasis in the middle of the barren high plain, and I felt ridiculous and humiliated having to leave in stealth and haste like a fugitive. But I had thought it over during the night, and as the German aphorist Lichtenberg pointed out, one should always follow the pillow's advice.

The cook saw me go out through the front door of the house and pretended to look in the other direction. When I got to the gate, I found it secured with a thick chain and a padlock. Luckily, the wall wasn't high and I had no trouble jumping it.

I had gone about a hundred metres when a truck pulled

over to the verge of the road.

"Where are you going?" asked one of the occupants of the cabin.

"To Barranco, to catch the air-taxi," I replied.

"If you don't mind company, you can ride in the back. We're going to Ibarra," said the driver.

"Fantastic. Thanks a lot," I said, and climbed up behind.

The truck was carrying several enormous pigs who greeted me as if I were one more of their number. Sitting in a corner on my pack, I thought of how I had been on the point of making the big break and getting to Europe, when life had forced me into yet another detour. To console myself, I concentrated on admiring the panorama of hills and ravines bathed in the intense glow of dawn on the high plain.

Suddenly, I felt that the pigs were staring at me. Someone, I don't remember who, said that pigs have a perverse gaze. Not these ones. They were watching me with innocent, frightened little eyes. Maybe they sensed that they were on their final journey.

"We have something in common, as I think you've already noticed. But I managed to escape in time. You, my friends, will end up as sausages. It's a pity, but hell, that's life."

Three weeks earlier I had been in Ambato, city of

flowers, rightly known as the home of the most beautiful women in Ecuador. I was heading for Coca, in the Amazon, with the intention of writing an article on the oil wells. As usual I was short of money, and a North American magazine had offered me a tidy sum for the job. In Ambato I was meant to meet up with an engineer who would take me as far as Cuenca in his jeep, and from there I was going to continue the journey in one of Texaco's light planes.

So there I was, on the terrace of a cafe, happily watching the girls who justify the city's reputation. Then, to rest my eyes from so much beauty, I glanced idly at the newspaper. There was an oddly worded advertisement:

Wanted: an educated young man, with good references, skilled in writing, to collaborate in compiling the memoirs of a distinguished public figure. Preference will be given to applicants of Spanish extraction. To make an appointment call . . .

My curiosity was tickled, so I rang. The phone was answered by a woman with a commanding voice, who ignored all my questions about the identity of the public figure but subjected me to a thorough interrogation, especially concerning my Spanish extraction. In the end, to my surprise, she told me I was accepted for the job, and mentioned in passing a fee that made me forget all about the article on the oil wells of Coca. Before ringing off, she explained how to get to the estate, which was about eight kilometres from Ambato, and added that she would expect me the following day.

Twenty-four hours later I knocked at the gate of La Conquistada, an impressive, rambling mansion in the colonial style, surrounded by gardens. In the entrance hall hung several dozen cages containing jungle birds, and there I was met by the woman who had spoken to me the day before on the telephone.

"They belong to my daughter. She loves birds. I hope the singing doesn't bother you in the mornings. The toucans are especially boisterous."

"Not at all. It's the best way to wake up."

"Come in. I'll show you your room."

Watching over the entrance was a life-sized standing portrait of an individual got up like Cortés, Almagro or any of those conquistadors. The warrior's hands rested on the hilt of his sword.

"The Governor Don Pedro de Sarmiento y Figueroa. We are his direct descendants, and proud of it," said the woman.

"What Spanish blood I have is not of such noble lineage," I remarked.

"All Spanish blood is noble," she replied.

The room she gave me was austere. The bed, the bedside table and the wardrobe made no secret of their antiquity. In the corner was a strange piece of furniture which at first I took to be a primitive clothes rack, but noticing the crucifix in front of it, I realised that it was a prie-dieu.

"For now make yourself comfortable. We'll expect you in the dining room in half an hour."

At lunch I observed that the descendants of the Governor were few, the last of the line.

The woman, who was a widow, ran the estate, and took real pleasure in humiliating the Indians who worked as servants and farm labourers. She had one daughter, Aparicia, who was about forty and moved awkwardly, as if apologising to the furniture for being nearly six feet tall and burdened with a body which, although well formed, was voluminous. From the moment I saw her, it seemed to me that she had stepped out of a baroque painting. The baroque masters painted short, full-bodied women. For some reason one of them slipped up and painted Aparicia, a great big full-bodied woman, and so as not to upset the school, he decided to take her out of the picture. Her face could have been beautiful, but it was spoilt by a grimace of bitterness or maybe even hate, inherited from her mother. Aparicia spent her days embroidering, and although I have always shrunk from zoological comparisons, when close to her I couldn't help noticing the characteristic sour-milk odour given off by females on heat. The head of the household was the distinguished public figure, the widow's father, who had been a player in the power struggles of the twenties. Like a character in a book by García Márquez he was known as the Colonel, and he lived on cassava pulp sweetened with palm syrup. Finally, there was Father Justiniano, an old priest who lurched around like a vulture sweating alcohol from every pore.

Life at La Conquistada was regulated by an inviolable routine. At seven in the morning I had to attend Mass in the family chapel. After breakfast, I chatted with the old colonel and the priest for a couple of hours. Then there was lunch, preceded by the saying of grace. In the afternoon, after the siesta, I would drink coffee with the two old men until it was time to say the rosary. After dinner we went into the lounge, where Aparicia embroidered, the old men played dominoes and the widow told me stories of the Governor's exploits.

One morning, when I had been there a week, I went into the entrance hall and found Aparicia talking to one of her birds. As soon as she realised I was there, the blood rushed to her cheeks and her breath came quick and halting. It seemed I had disturbed her in a moment of real intimacy, and I tried to put her at ease with a pleasant remark.

"You have very pretty birds. What is this one called?" I asked, pointing to a cage chosen at random.

"Bull bird," she replied, without looking at me.

"Can you make it sing?"

"It is best if that bird does not sing," she said, and went away, leaving an aroma of sour milk in the entrance hall.

I stayed there looking at the cage. The bird was about twenty-four centimetres long, with shiny blue-black plumage. It had a tuft of green and grey feathers on its head, and from its breast hung a ruff of feathers like those of the peacock. I lifted my hand, and the bird, frightened perhaps, puffed up its breast like a toad and made a sound totally alien to its fragile beauty. A coarse, uncouth sound, like the bellowing of cattle frightened by a storm.

A cleaning woman approached, pretending to dust the banister.

"Don't make that bird sing, sir. It's a very unlucky bird. Every time it sings in the jungle, the other birds go away and leave it alone. Poor thing. It's Miss Aparicia's favourite."

In the afternoons, the widow smiled with satisfaction to see me going through my notes, but I had begun to see the whole thing as a very well paid waste of time. The distinguished public figure's recollections turned out to have faded considerably as a result of arteriosclerosis and the priest's censorship. There was nothing left of the liberal he had been, and the poor old boy sometimes mixed up his own experiences with things he had read about. So it wasn't really surprising that he referred to the 1912 assassination of Eloy Alfaro as a consequence of the Napoleonic Wars.

After a fortnight, I was thinking that my stay at La Conquistada was the first holiday I had had for years. I was eating well, sleeping as never before, breathing the purest air and drinking Spanish wine. The widow filled me in on the profitable cattle business, and Aparicia made sure that my clothes were freshly washed and impeccably ironed. Sometimes that smell of a female on heat roused my blood, and I found myself thinking that after a couple of bottles I might risk visiting the embroiderer's bedroom.

Every morning, Aparicia sat next to me at Mass. I could never hear what she said as she knelt in front of the virgin sculpted by Capiscara, a family heirloom. But although I never heard her words, I could guess from her gestures that, far from praying, she was railing, berating and, who knows, maybe even cursing the God who had made her so tall and corpulent.

In those two weeks I filled a pair of notebooks with the Colonel's reminiscences and the priest's commentaries. Of all of them, the priest was the one who interested me the most. By rosary time, in the afternoon, he had already downed a couple of bottles of *caña*, and could no longer hold back the resentment he harboured towards the Amazon Indians. He called them savages, heretics and degenerates, accusing them of being his downfall. Gradually, his liquor-sodden features won me over, especially after the cook told me that in his youth he had been a missionary to the Aucas.

"He was a candidate for canonisation, but he just went crazy for those jungle women. Since they are all beautiful and they go around naked, he forgot about his vow of celibacy, and they say he had five children in the jungle. Then he went mad thinking that those poor bastards were out there somewhere: naked, eating raw meat and jumping from tree to tree like monkeys."

I tried to get the priest to talk, but the old soak was parsimonious with his words. When he had drunk so much *caña* that he couldn't stand up, the widow and Aparicia would take him off to bed on a stretcher. They would come back shortly afterwards, playing down the reverend father's dipsomania. The widow would offer me a glass of cognac and we would talk about the Colonel's memoirs, how long it would take to write them up and the happiness it would give her to see them published.

The night before my undignified departure from La Conquistada, the widow offered me a new job: this time my task would be to write the biography of the Governor. I was aflutter with emotion at this offer, because it included a trip to Europe.

"Naturally, you would have to travel to Spain in order to carry out research in the Archive of the Indies in Seville. But we'll talk about that when the Colonel's memoirs see the light of day."

I tossed and turned all that night; I couldn't sleep a wink. I was onto something good with that family, however much they gloried in their stupid nostalgia. Quite by chance I had happened on a real gold mine. For the first time in my life I was being respected and paid for what I had always wanted to do: writing. And, to crown my good fortune, they were going to send me off to Europe.

I felt like a glass of milk, so I left the bedroom and went to the kitchen. Standing next to the cook was a man I had seen breaking in a colt. He was dressed all in white, with a red handkerchief knotted around his neck, like a farmer from the coast.

While the cook heated up some milk on the stove, the guy looked me up and down, smiling rather cynically.

"I had to see it to believe it," he said, bursting into laughter.

"I'm really that funny, am I?"

"Don't flatter yourself. To be honest, I think you're an idiot."

"Hold it right there. I don't even know you and you're insulting me. Am I allowed to know why?"

"Don't say anything, José. Don't get yourself into trouble," was the cook's advice.

"Jesus! Somebody's got to tell him."

"Tell me what?"

Then the guy stood up, walked to the door, and from there beckoned me to follow him. Still dazed, I turned to the cook.

"Go with him, sir. It's incredible, but you have no idea what's going on."

We went out into the cold night of the high plain. With another gesture, the man indicated that we were going to the stables. When we got there, he gave me a box to sit on and passed me a bottle.

"Take a swig. I think you need it."

I drank. I could feel it destroying my guts. It was *puro*, the strongest cane liquor there is. I coughed and the guy tapped me on the back.

"Listen, I'm sorry I called you an idiot. It's just that you are."

"Whatever you say. Have you got a cigarette to help the poison go down?"

He took two long cigars from his shirt pocket, gave me one and, while he lit it, looked into my eyes as one looks at an imbecile.

"Well, come on then, out with it."

"They are fattening you up, my friend, like a pig."

"I don't understand a word of what you're saying."

"Lord have mercy on idiots. They are fattening you up, but not for the abattoir. They're going to marry you."

"What the hell are you talking about?"

"They're going to marry you. The widow has already decided that you are just the man for the big girl. You're single, you're not a local, you don't know anyone or have any family round here, and no offence, but like all literary types you probably live with your head in the clouds, so you'll never stick your nose into the widow's business dealings. You are husband material."

"You're crazy. Where did you get all this rubbish from?"

"It's obvious you're not from around here; if you were, you'd already have noticed what's going on. Think about it: at Mass they put you next to the big girl, at the dinner table they put you next to her too, and for the rosary, same place. And who washes and irons your clothes? She does. Who makes your bed and puts flowers in your room? She does. Have you noticed what she is embroidering? Sheets, my friend. Wedding sheets. No woman round here does that in the presence of a man unless he's her fiancé."

The farmer's words left me speechless. The cigar smoke was chafing my throat and I asked him to pass me the bottle again. This time the *puro* seemed less corrosive, and I began to discern a certain logic in the whole business.

"Suppose what you say is true. Why are you telling me all this?"

"Because I feel sorry for you. Look, there are plenty of us willing to marry that freak, for the estate, naturally. But since we have our pride, none of us is prepared to give up his name. Don't you see? They are grooming you to be the sire who saves the house of Sarmiento y Figueroa. The widow is a mad old woman, and like her father and the priest, she is determined to get the big girl pregnant so she can get one or more sons out of her to continue the line of the Governor, or whatever they call that Spanish shit. It's true that she's a widow, but before she became one, she spent her life cursing Aparicia's father, a man from Latacunga who left her, and for good reason. When Aparicia was born, that old bastard of a colonel had them both whipped for having engendered a female instead of the male they were hoping for. You see? And if you're wondering why the widow didn't have a child by some other man, the answer is simple: no-one with any Indian blood in his veins is fit to continue the Sarmiento y Figueroa line."

"I have Indian blood, from the Indians where I come from," I ventured to say.

"Well, the Indians there must be real idiots. Round here we know what's what. They're going to marry you. And you'd better get her pregnant quick smart, and woe betide you if she doesn't have a boy."

"And what if I refuse to get married?"

"Listen, my friend, no-one would want to be in the shoes of a foreigner who had dared to offend the owners of La Conquistada."

At dusk, the men in the truck dropped me off in Ibarra. After saying goodbye to them and the pigs, the first thing I did was to ring a friend who was a lawyer in Quito, to get his opinion on the matter.

"You've got yourself into a real fix. Those paranoiacs are unpredictable when their pride is wounded."

"It's absurd. The whole thing is absurd."

"In Ecuador, everything is so absurd that nothing comes as a surprise to anyone. The Sarmiento y Figueroa family is one of the forty that call the shots in this country. Make yourself scarce for a good long while."

I took my friend's advice. I travelled to Colombia, to Bogotá and from there to Cartagena de Indias. I don't know if the widow had my name put on a blacklist and I had forgotten the whole story, when some years later my travels brought me back to Ecuador. At the Otavalo market, I ran into the cook from La Conquistada.

The good lady was no longer at the estate; she was working as a street vendor, selling roast guinea pigs. She offered me a little wicker chair and, after treating me to the plumpest of her tasty rodents, told me how the story ended.

"When they found out that you had run away, the widow and the two old guys gave Miss Aparicia a terrible beating. They hit her and shouted at her, saying she was a fool not to have got into your bed in those three weeks. In the end, the poor thing, all battered and covered with bruises, still had the strength left to kill the birds in the cages. She left just one alive. A black jungle bird that made a noise like a cow. I was sorry for Miss Aparicia, but I was happy for you."

"And then what happened?"

"Four or five months later another young man came to write the Colonel's memoirs. A young man who spoke funny. He said something like *'Obrigado'* every time I served him something."

"A Brazilian. It doesn't matter. Please go on."

"They married him to Miss Aparicia. It finally worked out for them."

"And . . .?"

"That's it. Now there's a boy at the estate. Do you know what he's called? Pedrito de Sarmiento y Figueroa," said the cook, with one of those wonderful smiles that belong only to the women of Otavalo.

Part Three

Notes from a Return Journey

Chapter One

"WELL, HERE we are," I say to myself, and a seagull turns its head to look at me for a few seconds. "Another crackpot," the gull must be thinking, because in fact I am on my own, facing the sea in Chonchi, a port on the big island of Chiloé, in the far south of the world.

I am waiting for the order to board *El Colono*, a ferry painted red and white, which after having plied the Baltic, Mediterranean and Adriatic seas for several decades, has come to float in the cold, deep and unpredictable waters of the South.

Supposedly, after twenty-four hours on *El Colono* – though the trip can take thirty or more, it all depends on the whims of the sea and the wind – I will disembark eight hundred kilometres further south, in the heart of Chilean Patagonia.

While waiting, I think about those two old gringos who pulled the flimsy strings of destiny that brought Bruce Chatwin and me together one winter midday on the terrace of the Cafe Zurich in Barcelona.

An Englishman and a Chilean. With not even an affection for the sound of the word 'homeland' in common. The Englishman a nomad because he could be nothing else, and the Chilean an exile for just the same reason. There should definitely be a law against encounters of this kind or, at the very least, they should not be allowed to take place in the presence of minors.

At the initiative of Bruce's Spanish publisher, the meeting had been arranged for midday and I arrived right on time. The Englishman was there already; he had settled down with a beer to read one of the perverse *El Víbora* comics. To attract his attention I tapped on the table. The Englishman raised his head and took a sip before speaking.

"I can put up with a punctual South American, but a man who has lived in Germany for several years and doesn't bring flowers when meeting someone for the first time is simply intolerable."

"If you like, I'll come back in a quarter of an hour with some flowers," I replied.

With a gesture he invited me to take a seat. I sat down, lit a cigarette, and we looked at each other without saying a word. He knew that I knew about the gringos, and I knew that he knew about them too.

"Are you from Patagonia?" he asked, breaking the silence.

"No, from further north."

"Just as well. You can't believe a quarter of what the Patagonians tell you. They're the world's greatest liars," he remarked, reaching for his beer. I felt obliged to hit back.

"That's because they learnt to lie from the English. Do you know the lies Fitzroy dreamed up for poor Jimmy Button?"

"One all!" said Bruce, and he reached out to shake my hand.

The preliminaries having reached a satisfactory conclusion, we got to talking about those old gringos, who were watching us from some place not marked on the maps, pleased to be witnesses to our encounter.

Several years have passed since that midday in Barcelona. Several years and several hours, because now, as I wait for the stevedores to finish loading *El Colono* and let me climb aboard, it is three in the afternoon of a February day, like that day years ago. Officially, it is summer in the southern hemisphere, but the icy wind off the Pacific is quite unperturbed by a minor detail like that; it is blowing in gusts that numb to the bone and force you to take refuge in the warmth of memories.

The two gringos we talked about in Barcelona were in the banking business for a good part of their working lives. It is well known that there are two ways of practising the business: being a banker and robbing banks. They opted for the second because, after all, they were gringos and true to the charitable puritanism of their forefathers, which urged them to share out the wealth obtained by robbery without delay. They shared it with actresses in Baltimore, opera singers in New York, Chinese cooks in San Francisco, chocolate-brown prostitutes in the brothels of Kingston and Havana, witches and soothsayers in La Paz, poets of doubtful merit in Santa Cruz, melancholic muses in Buenos Aires, sailors' widows in Punta Arenas, and they ended up financing impossible revolutions in Patagonia and Tierra del Fuego. They were called Robert Leroy Parker and Harry Longabaugh, Mister Wilson and Mister Evans, Billy and Jack, Don Pedro and Don José. They set off across the infinite plains of legend as Butch Cassidy and the Sundance Kid.

I remember all this as I wait, sitting on a wine barrel, facing the sea, in the far south, and I make notes in a notebook with square-ruled paper, which Bruce gave me especially for this trip. It's not just any notebook. It's a museum piece: an authentic *moleskine*, of the kind preferred by writers such as Céline and Hemingway, and no longer stocked by stationers. Bruce suggested that before using it I should do what he did: first number the pages, then write at least two contact addresses inside the front cover and, finally, promise a reward to whoever returns the book if it is lost. When I remarked that all this seemed excessively English, Bruce replied that it was just this kind of precautionary measure that had allowed the English to preserve the illusion that they had an empire; with blood and fire they inscribed the idea of belonging to England in each colony, and when they lost the colonies, in exchange for a small economic reward they got them back again as members of what is euphemistically called the British Commonwealth of Nations.

The *moleskines* were handmade by a bookbinder in Tours, as they had been by his family since the early days of the twentieth century, but when he died, none of his descendants wanted to continue the tradition. There is no point lamenting their end. It is just another consequence of so-called modernity, which day by day eliminates rites, customs and details we will soon remember with nostalgia.

A voice announces that the boat will weigh anchor 'in a few minutes', but it doesn't say how many.

The majority of the little ports and villages of Chiloé were founded by pirates, or as a defence against them, in the sixteenth and seventeenth centuries. Pirates or gentle-

87

men, they all had to go through the Strait of Magellan and consequently stop in places like Chonchi to stock up with provisions. The utilitarian character of the buildings goes back to that time: they all have two functions, though one is more important. The various establishments serve as bar and blacksmith's shop, bar and post office, bar and shipping agent, bar and funeral parlour. I go into one which is a bar and animal dispensary, but a sign hanging on the door affirms that it has yet another function: ANIMALS AND HUMANS TREATED FOR MANGE AND DIARRHOEA.

I sit myself down at a table, near the window. At the tables nearby they are playing *truco*, a card game which allows all sorts of facial signals between partners and requires you to accompany the cards you play with properly rhyming verses. I order a glass of wine.

"A glass or a half?" asks the waiter.

I was born in this country, just a bit further to the north. It is scarcely two thousand kilometres from Chonchi to the city of my birth, but perhaps in my long absence from these parts I have forgotten certain important distinctions. Without thinking, I insist on having a glass.

A little while later the waiter comes back with an enormous glass that holds nearly a litre. You have to watch the units of measurement in the far south.

Good wine. A *pipeño*: young, slightly acid, rough, wild like the country awaiting me beyond this port. It goes down well, and as it does, a story that Bruce especially liked to tell comes back to me.

Once, on the way back from Patagonia, with his pack full of the *moleskine* notebooks in which he had set down the raw material for what would later be entitled *In Patagonia*, one of the best travel books ever written, Bruce was passing through Cucao, in the eastern part of the island. He had gone hungry for days, so he wanted to eat, but without putting too much of a strain on his stomach.

"I would like something light, please," he told the waiter.

They served him half a leg of roast lamb, and when he complained, insisting that he had wanted something light, he was given one of those answers that leave you speechless:

"It was a very thin lamb, sir. You wouldn't find a lighter one anywhere on the island."

Curious people. And since Chiloé is the anteroom of Patagonia, here begin the beautiful and ingenuous eccentricities we will see and hear further to the south. An Argentinian teacher told me a priceless story. One of his students wrote the following about clocks: 'We use clocks to weigh delays. Clocks break down too, and just as cars lose oil, clocks lose time'.

Did somebody mention the death of surrealism?

The port is beginning to bustle. The big trucks are already on board, and now the smaller vehicles are going on. Soon they will call for the passengers, once the stevedores have finished transporting the cargo. These islanders are vigorous. Stocky men, with short but solid legs, they trot along carrying heavy sacks of potatoes and vegetables, bolts of cloth, kitchen utensils, boxes of salt, sacks of maté, tea and sugar: merchandise that belongs to retailers, mostly the sons or grandsons of Lebanese immigrants, who, when they disembark with their droves of horses, will do the rounds of the ranches and tiny isolated towns in the mountains, beside the fiords or out on the endless pampa.

I finish the wine. The movement around me is contagious and my whole body is eager to get going.

This is a journey that began several years back, it doesn't matter how many. It began that cold February day in Barcelona, sitting with Bruce at a table outside the Cafe Zurich. The two old gringos kept us company, but only we could see them. There were four of us at the table, so it shouldn't come as a shock to anyone that we emptied two bottles of cognac.

Perhaps we will never find out how those two bandits organised their bank robberies, but I can tell you how an Englishman and a Chilean, pretty drunk at about five in the afternoon, planned a journey to the end of the earth.

"So, Mister Púlveda, when are we leaving?"

"Just as soon as they let me go back, Mister Win."

"So you still have problems with the apes who run your country?"

"I don't. They're the ones who have problems with me."

"I see. It doesn't matter. It just gives us more time to prepare the journey."

And they went on talking about other matters of minor importance, such as finding the ranch where Butch Cassidy and the Sundance Kid are supposed to have been decapitated, visiting the grave where they say the two adventurers lie buried, imaginatively reconstructing the last days of their lives and, finally, in four-handed collaboration, filling up the pages of a saga or a novel.

When I finally got the long-awaited permission to return to the far south, Bruce Chatwin had already set off on the ineluctable journey. It strikes me that when he bought up the entire existing stock of *moleskines* in an old Parisian stationer's in the Rue de l'Ancienne Comédie, the only place that sold them, Bruce was unwittingly preparing himself for the long, last journey. What could he have noted in them, wherever he is?

The permission to return to my country took me by surprise in Hamburg. For nine years I had visited the

Chilean consulate every Monday to see if I could go back. In that time I was told the same thing about five hundred times: "No, your name is on the list of those who cannot return."

Then, suddenly, one Monday in January the dreary official broke with his routine and upset my habit of listening to his definite negatives: "Whenever you like, you can return whenever you like. Your name has been taken off the list."

I left the consulate shaking. I sat by the Alster for hours before I remembered that promises made to friends are sacred, and decided to set off for the end of the earth within a few days.

At last they call the passengers. Here we go, Bruce, doomed Englishman, though you'll have to travel as a stowaway, hidden between the pages of the *moleskine*. By tomorrow night we'll be in Patagonia, on the trail of those two gringos who inspired this adventure, and neither they nor the gauchos you knew will be surprised to see us arrive, because in the intense solitude of their ranches, the Patagonians affirm that 'death begins when a person accepts that he has died'.

El Colono has cast off its moorings, but the gangplank is still being raised. Two members of the crew are arguing with an old man, white as a sheet, who is insisting on bringing a coffin aboard. The crew members object that it is unlucky. The old man replies that he has a right to seventy kilos of luggage. The sailors threaten to chuck the casket overboard. The old man yells that he has cancer, and that he has a right to a decent burial, because he is a gentleman. Finally, the captain intervenes and an agreement is reached: they will take him and his coffin as long as he promises not to die during the trip. The deal is sealed with a handshake. Then the old man sits down on his coffin. All this is food for the *moleskine*.

The boat begins to move, pointing its prow towards Golfo Corcovado. Soon it will be dark, and it is comforting to know that I have a canteen full of vigorous *pipeño* wine and plenty of tobacco. I am ready to store up everything I see in the notebook. Soon we will be sailing under the southern stars towards the end of the world.

When by the light of the Southern Cross I drink to the health of the doomed Englishman who set off first, the wind seems to bring me an echo of hoofbeats: the sound of two old gringos galloping along an uncertain shoreline, in a region so vast and so full of adventures that it cannot be limited by the petty border separating life from death.

Chapter Two

A T THE mouth of the great fiord of Aisén, *El Colono* decelerates to make the forty-five-degree turn that will allow it to enter Patagonia. Our progress becomes very slow, almost monotonous, like the movements of the truck drivers travelling on the ferry, who kill time playing games of dominoes, drinking bitter maté or shaving in front of the rear-vision mirrors of their vehicles. Others, who are not playing or grooming themselves, check that the loads on the trucks haven't shifted, that the sacks of garlic, potatoes, onions, other vegetables and all the things that can't be grown, ripened or manufactured in the vast region to which they are heading are secure on the backs of the trucks, which rest like sleeping animals in the belly of a red and white whale.

The dawn is still; just the slightest breeze to let us know that we are leaving the Pacific and going into the quiet waters of the great fiord. Its surface looks like a metal plate, silver where the rising sun glints off it.

On the bridge, the helmsman and two officers intently scrutinise the quiet path of water. Seamen like the fiord when it is choppy. From the movement of the water they can spot the treacherous sand banks and sharp reefs hidden below the surface. Nothing worse than a flat sea, sailors often say in the South. We are heading south-west, and with a bit of luck we will be able to dock at a place called Trapananda.

"How do we get to Trapananda?" I ask a truck driver.

"I don't have the slightest idea. The captain might know," he replies, without interrupting his shave.

No. Definitely not a Patagonian.

I persist. "How do we get to Trapananda?" I ask one of those drinking maté.

"By taking it easy, my friend. Nice and easy," he answers, observing me with an expression of complicity.

Yes. Definitely a Patagonian.

Trapananda. In 1570 the governor of Chile, Don García Hurtado de Mendoza, concluded, much to his regret, that the rumours of large deposits of gold and silver south of La Frontera, in the region overlooked by Cerro Ñielol, from

95

which the Mapuche, Pehuenche and Tehuelche Indians – America's first guerrilla fighters – had launched a war of resistance which would last for more than four centuries, were just that: rumours based on deceit.

Don García Hurtado de Mendoza wasn't particularly interested in precious metals. He was a farmer, and like many other Castilian conquistadors, including Pedro de Valdivia, he had realised, to his great satisfaction, that the agricultural potential of the land to the north of the river Biobío was infinite. Everything grew there. You just had to scatter seeds and the fertile soil did the rest.

Even wine grapes grew well. In 1562, the land granted to the concession-holder Jerónimo de Urmeneta, twenty leagues south of Santiago del Nuevo Extremo, produced the first fifty barrels of Chilean wine. It was a thick broth, strong, dry and dark as the night. A good wine to consecrate, but better to drink. The descendants of the concession-holder went on making it, and these days Urmeneta del Valle del Maipo is considered one of the planet's finest wines.

Everything grew on that land, but what they wanted back in Spain was silver and gold, so Don García decided once again to admit that there might be some truth in the rumours of rich gold or silver deposits.

This time the soldiers had been talking about a mysterious kingdom of Tralalanda, Trapalanda or Trapananda, where the cities were paved with gold ingots and the doors of the houses swung open on large hinges of the purest silver. Some even declared that Tralalanda, Trapalanda or Trapananda was none other than the mythical Lost City of the Caesars, a sort of southern El Dorado. And the rumours affirmed that this marvellous kingdom extended south from Reloncaví, about twelve hundred kilometres from the newly founded Chilean capital.

So Don García Hurtado de Mendoza organised an expedition, under the command of the provincial governor Arias Pardo Maldonado, and sent him off with orders to conquer for Spain the kingdom of Tralalanda, Trapalanda or Trapananda, or whatever the hell it was called.

No historian has been able to find out for sure whether or not Arias Pardo Maldonado ever got beyond Reloncaví and into continental Patagonia, but some documents in his handwriting are conserved in the Archives of the Indies in Seville:

> *The inhabitants of Trapananda are tall, monstrous and hairy. Their feet are so enormous that they walk slowly and awkwardly, and are thus easy targets for the arquebusiers.*
>
> *The Trapanandans have ears so large that they can cover their bodies with them when they sleep and so have*

no need of blankets or other coverings.

The Trapanandans give off such a pestilential odour that they cannot stand one another's presence, and for this reason, they do not approach one another, couple or have offspring.

What does it matter whether or not Arias Pardo Maldonado found the kingdom of Trapananda, whether or not he reached Patagonia? He marks the beginning of the tradition of American fantastic literature and of our disproportionate imagination, and that is enough to legitimate his stature as a historical figure.

Perhaps he did reach Patagonia, and, seduced by its landscapes, he invented those stories of monstrous beings to keep other possible explorers away. If that was his intention, it could be said that he succeeded, since Chilean Patagonia remained virgin land until the beginning of this century, when its colonisation began.

We have gone eight kilometres into Patagonia when *El Colono* slows down again. Along with some other passengers I lean over the handrail to see what is going on. With a bit of luck it is still possible to see a whale or a school of southern dolphins migrating. This time, however, it is not sea mammals, but a boat, coming more clearly into view as it approaches.

It is a skiff from Chiloé. A little boat about eight metres

long and three across, pushed along by the breeze that fills out its single sail. I watch it approach and I know that this flimsy boat is part of what was calling me from the far south.

"He who dares, eats," say the inhabitants of Chiloé. This man, sitting on the stern of his skiff, with the rudder blade firmly under control, as if it were an extension of his body that went down over the edge of the stern and into the water, is one of the men from Chiloé who 'dared' to raise oaks, larches, poplars, eucalypts and teaks, guiding their growth for long years, hanging stones of varying weights on them until the trunks attained the maturity and curvature required to make strong and springy boat timbers. I watch him as he sails past and, with a gesture, thanks the captain for having given the order to slow down so *El Colono*'s wake will not rock the little boat too much. Now he is sailing down the great fiord, but I know he also plies the Golfo Corcovado, the terrible Golfo de Penas, the Canales de Messier, the Canales del Indio, the Strait of Magellan and the open sea, without radar, without radio, with nothing more, and nothing less, than his knowledge of the sea and the winds.

This sea-wanderer is my brother, and he is the first to welcome me to Patagonia.

Chapter Three

LADISLAO EZNAOLA and his younger brothers, Iñaqui and Agustín, built their ranch's main homestead on the north shore of a lake which is called General Carrera in Chile and Buenos Aires on the Argentinian side of the border. About a thousand head of cattle and five thousand sheep graze on their six-thousand-hectare property. They make a living from stockbreeding and trading in other products shipped down from the north of Chile, which they transport in sturdy *chatas* (trucks with a high hauling capacity), and then in the two ferries they run on the lake.

The inhabitants of Perito Moreno and other towns in Argentinian Patagonia welcome the Eznaolas' ferries with relief, especially during the long winter months, when the roads become impassable and the locals stop receiving supplies from Puerto Deseado and Comodoro Rivadavia, towns on the Atlantic coast.

Ladislao greets me with a wholehearted hug, and I ask after his father, the legendary Old Eznaola.

"He's still doing his thing. He hasn't changed. Never will. And he's eighty-two now," he informs me, half amused, half worried.

'His thing' is navigation. Old Eznaola is another sea-wanderer, but not like those from Chiloé. He plies the canals looking for a ghost ship, which might be the *Caleuche*, a southern version of the *Flying Dutchman*, or the *Cacafuego* ('*Shitfire*'), an English pirate ship condemned to wander eternally up and down the canals without ever being able to reach the open sea, held captive by a curse which the members of the crew brought upon themselves when they mutinied and killed two captains. This curse has lasted more than four hundred years, and it is Old Eznaola's opinion that the poor fellows have suffered enough. That is why he searches the canals in his cutter, flying amnesty pennants. He wants to offer his expert services and pilot them to the vast freedom of the sea.

"There you go. Spoil yourself," says Marta, Ladislao's wife, handing me a plate with two *empanadas* on it.

I greet the women of the ranch. Marta is a vet; Isabel,

Iñaqui's wife, is a teacher, and looks after the education of the new generation of Eznaolas and the other children on the ranch. Flor, Agustín's wife, is a legend in Patagonia. She used to work as a nurse in the hospital at Río Mayo in Argentina. Agustín had always been in love with her, but had never dared to tell her how he felt. He saw her once a year, and after every visit his love became so intense it almost suffocated him. One day he found out that Flor was going to marry a bank clerk. He climbed into his *chata* with a guitar and asked his brothers and sisters-in-law to spruce up the house because he was going to come back with the woman of his dreams.

He arrived at Río Mayo on the Sunday of the wedding, and with his guitar at the ready, he took up his position in the church to wait for the woman he loved. Flor appeared in her wedding dress, accompanied by her parents. The groom was expected shortly. Agustín asked her to listen to him, without saying anything, until the arrival of the groom. Then he strummed his guitar and launched into verses in which he expressed his love with all the beauty poetry could lend and all the pain of a man whose devotion would last unto death and beyond. When the groom arrived he wanted to interrupt the singer, but Flor and the villagers of Río Mayo wouldn't let him. Agustín sang for two hours and, finally, when he was about to break his guitar so that nobody could profane his love song, Flor took him by the hand, led him to the *chata* and together they set out for the ranch. Flor arrived in her wedding dress, and since then Agustín, who is one of the region's best poets, has called her 'my white muse'.

"And how's Don Baldo Araya?" I ask, worried by the absence of one of my best Patagonian friends.

"He won't be long. He's coming with the guys from the radio. Everyone else is here. Come and meet them," says Ladislao.

"Santos Gamboa, from Río Mayo."

"At your service," says the man in question, lifting two fingers to the rim of his gaucho hat.

"Do you still have that music in Río Mayo?" I ask him.

The gaucho scratches the back of his neck before replying in the affirmative.

Río Mayo is a small town in Argentinian Patagonia, perpetually swept by a strong wind from the Atlantic that drags tumbleweeds, tangles of grass and tons of dust across the pampa. You usually can't see the other side of the street for dust in Río Mayo.

In 1977, during the military dictatorship in Argentina, a colonel of the Chubut Fusiliers had a brilliant idea – militarily speaking, that is – for preventing possible gatherings of conspirators in the streets. At every street corner he hung loudspeakers from the lampposts and used them to bombard the town with military 'music' – for want of a better term – from 7 a.m. to 7 p.m. When Argentina joined the group of nations with probationary democracies, the new authorities refused to remove the loudspeakers for fear of ruffling the military, and the inhabitants of Río Mayo went on being subjected to a daily twelve-hour noise bombardment. Since 1977, the birds of Patagonia have steered clear of the town and the majority of the locals have hearing problems.

Ladislao continues with the introductions: "Lorenzo Urriola, from Perito Mayo. Carlos Hainz, from Coihaique. Marcos Santelices, from Chile Chico. Isidoro Cruz, from Las Heras."

"It's getting late. I think we should start. Baldo and the guys from the radio will miss the first part," says Iñaqui, passing me a melon cut open at one end; it's had its flesh scraped out and replaced with refreshing white wine.

Some farmhands bring forward a lamb to inaugurate the castration of the animals which aren't going to be used for reproduction, whose only purpose will be to grow fat and produce kilos and more kilos of meat.

The first lamb is for Marcos Santelices. Two helpers throw it onto a board and hold its back legs open so that Santelices, having checked the edge on his silver-handled gaucho knife, can shave off the fine down that covers the testicles of the frightened animal. When the skin is pink and clean, Santelices stabs the knife into the table and leans forward, putting his head between the animal's thighs. Delicately, he takes the testicles in one hand, while with the other he feels for the veins in the enveloping bag of skin. When he finds them, he squeezes hard to cut off the flow of blood and rips the scrotum with his teeth.

Nobody notices the testicles going into Santelices's mouth, but then we see him take a few steps back and spit them into a basin, while the helpers tie up the empty, useless bag to prevent bleeding. Everyone is impressed by the skill of the gaucho from Chile Chico. Lambs castrated 'dentally' shouldn't lose a single drop of blood.

About twelve animals have already met with the gelders' teeth, and we are devouring delicious roast testicles, when we see a jeep approaching, emblazoned with the slogan: RADIO GLACIER, THE VOICE OF PATAGONIA.

The first person I see get out is Baldo Araya, the famously obstinate teacher at the Coihaique high school and an expert on Patagonian history, who, during the grey years of the military dictatorship in Chile, refused to sing the verses the gorillas added to the national anthem. Each Monday, all the students and teachers intoned the revolting 'Your names, courageous soldiers, pillars of the fatherland . . .'. All of

105

them except Baldo Araya, who remained silent. They beat him, they put him in jail for several months, accusing him of contempt, but they didn't succeed in bending his will. Finally, they decided to have him sacked, but one morning, in front of the quarters of the Baquedano regiment, one of the guard dogs was found with its throat cut and a note in its muzzle: 'Don't you see you're surrounded, cretins? You in the barracks and us outside. Leave Mister Araya alone'.

They didn't get him sacked, but they cut off his salary. It didn't matter to Baldo; he went on giving his classes on world history. For fourteen years he was supported by the sturdy solidarity of the Patagonians. He was never without a cask of wine or chickens to lay him brown eggs or meat for Sunday roasts.

"I was the happy recipient of the village scholarship," Baldo said to me a couple of years ago, in conclusion to his story.

Also among those in the jeep is Jorge Díaz – broadcaster, manager, programmer, researcher, disc jockey and technician for Radio Glacier. In 1972 Jorge Díaz – sometime sportscaster, truck driver, marine fisherman, miner and tango singer – had the idea of setting up a radio station unlike all others broadcasting to the far south. A station for those cut off from the world and even from their neighbours, especially during the long winters, without road links, telephones or mail. With his savings and those of a couple of friends, he bought second-hand equipment, set it up, obtained a broadcasting licence and began to transmit in the long-wave band.

'Patagonia Calling', a two-hour programme, quickly became the most popular. It transmitted useful announcements: 'A message to the Moran family, of Lake Cochrane. Don Evaristo is on his way. Have fresh horses ready for him: he's travelling with friends and lots of luggage'; or 'The Braun family, of Lake Elizalde, invites all the inhabitants of the region and the people listening to this programme to a party to celebrate the marriage of its eldest son, Octavio Braun, to Miss Faumelinda Brautigam. There will be *truco* and knucklebones championships, breaking-in of colts, roast lamb, pork and beef. There will also be poetry recitals, organised by Santos de la Roca, the bard of Río Gallegos. Please bring tents to sleep in. The party will last a week.'

In 1976 the military government started sending political prisoners into exile in Patagonia. The letters that the exiles received or sent to their families in the North were all subjected to military censorship, which usually meant destroying them. So Radio Glacier, the Voice of Patagonia, started transmitting messages on short wave, and the exiles not only communicated with their families in this way, they also broadcast political programmes. Within a few months, Radio Glacier was being received even in Arica, on the Peruvian border, nearly four thousand kilometres away.

The reaction of the military government was not long in coming. One night the transmission tower was blown up by 'unidentified agents' after the curfew. But the Patagonians were not so easily discouraged: as often as he needed them, Jorge Díaz was supplied with the longest and the most flexible eucalypt trunks to rebuild the antenna. And he went on transmitting. As he still does, and will continue to.

Ladislao Eznaola calls those present to silence by hitting his knife against the grill.

"Fellow countrymen, continuing a tradition on our ranch, we are going to open the Eighteenth Patagonian Lying Championship. All the lies told here will be broadcast later on Radio Glacier. Jorge Díaz will record them, so don't be afraid of the microphone. As in the previous competitions, the prize for the winner is a Holstein calf."

Where else in the world would you find a tournament like this, a tournament of lies?

Isidoro Cruz, from Las Heras in the province of Chubut, takes a long draught of wine before beginning.

"I'm going to tell you about something that happened

some time ago, in the year of the terrible winter, I'm sure you remember it. I was poor and thin. So thin I didn't cast a shadow, so thin I couldn't wear a poncho, because as soon as I put my head through the hole, the poncho fell straight down to my feet. One morning, I said to myself: 'Isidoro, things can't go on like this, there's nothing for it, you're going to Chile.' My horse was as thin as I was, so before mounting him I said to him: 'Listen, hack, do you think you can carry me?' 'Yes,' he replied, 'but not with the saddle too. Just sit yourself between my ribs.' I took the horse's advice and together we set out to cross the mountains. I was approaching the Chilean border when, from some-where close by, I heard a feeble, feeble voice saying: 'I can't go on, I'm staying here.' I looked around everywhere in fright, trying to find the owner of the voice, but saw no-one. So I said, to no-one: 'I can't see you. Show your-self.' The feeble voice made itself heard once more: 'In your left armpit. I'm in your left armpit.' I reached into my loose hide and felt something between the wrinkles of my armpit. When I pulled my hand out, there was a louse clinging to my finger, a louse as thin as my horse and myself. Poor louse, I thought, and I asked him how long he had been living on my body. 'Many, many years. But the time has come to go our separate ways. Although I don't weigh a gram, I am a useless burden to you and your horse.

Leave me on the ground, my friend.' I felt that the louse was right, and I left him hidden under a stone so that he wouldn't be eaten by some mountain bird. 'If things go well for me in Chile, I'll look for you on the way back and you can bite me all you like,' I said, bidding him goodbye.

"In Chile, things went well for us. I put on weight, the horse fattened up too, and when, after a year, we set out for home with money to spend, a saddle and new spurs, I looked for the louse where I had left him. He was there: even thinner, almost transparent, and hardly able to move. 'Hey, louse, here I am, come and bite, bite all you like,' I said, putting him in my left armpit. And the louse bit me, slowly at first, then vigorously, thirsty for blood. Suddenly, the louse began to laugh, and I laughed too, and my laugh infected the horse. We crossed the mountains laughing, drunk with happiness, and since then that pass through the mountains has been called the Pass of Happiness. All this happened, as I told you, some time ago, in the year of the terrible winter . . ."

Isidoro Cruz finishes his lie with a straight face. The gauchos consider the various parts of the story, evaluate them, decide that it's a fine lie, applaud, drink, and promise not to forget it; then it's time to hear Carlos Hainz, a blond gaucho from Coihaique.

As night falls, the gauchos go on telling their lies beside

the campfire. Farm labourers roast a pair of lambs. The ladies of the ranch announce that dinner is served. Baldo Araya and I decide to make a brief visit to the blackberries.

There, urinating copiously, I lift my head to look at the sky studded with stars, thousands of stars.

"Nice lie, that one about the louse," says Baldo.

"And this sky? All these stars, Baldo? Are they another Patagonian lie?"

"What does it matter? Down here we lie to be happy. But we all know the difference between lying and deception."

Chapter Four

LOS ANTIGUOS is a little border town on the southern shore of Lake Buenos Aires in Argentinian Patagonia. The smooth hillsides sloping down to the water bear pitiful witness to a grandeur which is just a memory now. They are littered with the remains of thousands of fallen giants, the vestiges of three hundred thousand hectares of forest, razed by fire to satisfy the graziers' need for pastures. The diameters of some of the remaining trunks exceed the height of a man.

Pablo Casorla is a forester who lives in Los Antiguos and is working on a survey of the forests that still exist in the region. He dreams of a forest reserve under the protection of UNESCO – another green item on the World Heritage List – to help future generations imagine what the whole area must have been like before the arrival of so-called progress. I see him get off his horse to examine a trunk.

"This tree was between eight hundred and a thousand years old. It must have been seventy metres high," he says, without trying to hide the sorrow in his voice.

"Do you know when it was burnt?"

"It'd be thirty years ago, more or less."

Thirty years. A recent death. Thirty years is hardly the time of a breath in the lives of the conquered giants that surround us, still bearing the scars left by fire.

"Is it much further?" I ask him.

"We're just about there. That's the cabin," he replies, pointing to a building not far off.

As we approach, I see just how massive the logs used to construct it are. It has no door and the window frames look like empty sockets. Without getting off the horses, we go into a large outbuilding with a stone fireplace against one wall. There are a few cows inside, chewing their cuds, and they look at us with languid eyes, as if accustomed to punishing the presumptuous strangers who blunder into their social club with indifference. In deference to the cows, we dismount.

"They built it in 1913. They were good carpenters, those guys. Look how well hewn the beams are," says Pablo Casorla.

And indeed the blackened beams that hold up the roof bear witness to the craftsmanship of hands skilled in the use of the gouge and the jack plane, and in the art of precise joinery.

The men who built the cabin went by the names of Don Pedro and Don José, but it is now known that they were really called Butch Cassidy and the Sundance Kid. They built several cabins in the far south, and the best known is on the outskirts of Cholila, in an area of ancient forest known as Los Alerces National Park. The present owner of the cabin is a Chilean, Doña Hermelinda Sepúlveda, who once put up Bruce Chatwin during his wanderings through the region and tried to marry him to one of her daughters, but the girl was swayed by the amorous pleas of a truck driver.

"The two men lived here for just over two years, then they moved further south, near Fuerte Bulnes on the Strait of Magellan. That's where they organised their last big robbery, the raid on the Bank of London and Tarapacá, in Punta Arenas. I wish they were still alive," says Pablo Casorla with a sigh.

"Alive? They would be more than a hundred years old!"

"So what? The leopard can never change its spots. If those two were still alive, I'd join them in a couple of robberies and we'd buy half of Patagonia with the loot.

What a pity they're dead." Pablo sighs again, and under the superior gaze of the cows, we drink a few draughts of wine to the health of those outlaws who were finally shot down by a Chilean policeman, after robbing banks throughout the far south and using the money to finance beautiful, impossible anarchist revolutions.

Chapter Five

IN THE middle of March the days start getting shorter, and strong winds from the Atlantic blow along the Strait of Magellan. This means it is time for the inhabitants of Porvenir to check their stocks of firewood and sadly watch the bustards crossing from Tierra del Fuego to Patagonia.

I had intended to go on to Ushuaia, but they tell me that several sections of the road have been washed away by the recent rains and won't be repaired until spring. It doesn't matter. It is absurd to have fixed plans in this part of the world, and anyway I'm quite happy here in El Austral, a seaman's bar known for its superlative lamb stew. Magallanes lamb, scented by the cloves hidden in the hearts of the onions that garnish it.

A dozen of us are on tenterhooks waiting for the proprietor to announce that dinner is served, drinking wine to pass the time as the aromas emanating from the kitchen torment us. There is a liturgical quality to this waiting that fills our mouths with saliva.

Three men are talking at one end of the bar. They are speaking a very British English while downing glasses of gin. It's not a very popular drink in Tierra del Fuego, and is more often used as a substitute for aftershave. One of the men asks in Spanish if dinner will be long.

"Hard to tell. Every lamb is different, like every person," replies the proprietor, Doña Sonia Marincovich, one metre eighty tall and about ninety kilos of Slavic humanity well distributed under her black dress.

"We don't have much time," insists the Englishman.

"The only thing we have too much of round here is time," remarks one of the patrons.

"We have to push off while there is still light, you see?"

"I see. And where are you headed? I ask because a donkey won't be able to stand up in the wind that's going to blow this afternoon."

"We're going to Raul's Cove."

"You must mean Incest Cove," corrects the patron.

The man thumps the bar with his hand, throws down a couple of bills for the drinks and goes out with his two companions, cursing in English.

I approach the patron who spoke with the irate Briton.

"Seems like he took offence. What was that about Incest Cove?"

"History, but the English have no sense of humour. Well, bugger them. They missed out on the stew. You don't know the story?"

I tell him I don't, and he steals a glance at Doña Sonia. From among her pots, she replies with a gesture of approval.

"Well, this is more or less how it happened. Round about 1935, a British steamship was wrecked in the Beagle Canal, and it seems that the only survivors were a Protestant missionary and his sister. The two castaways could have walked eastwards and in a week they would have got to Ushuaia, but since they had no sense of direction they walked north. They went about eighty kilometres through forests, crossing rivers, up and down hills, and finally, after four months, they turned up at what, until then, had been called Raul's Cove, on the south side of Almirantazgo Sound. There they were found by some Tehuelche Indians, who guided them to Porvenir. That's the story."

"So why is the place called Incest Cove now?"

"Because when they got there the woman was pregnant. To her brother."

"Come and sit down. Dinner's ready," announces Doña

Sonia, and we give ourselves over body and soul to the enjoyment of the excellent lamb stew the Englishmen missed out on because of their grumpiness.

Chapter Six

To the north of Manantiales, an oil town in Tierra del Fuego, stand the twelve or fifteen houses of a little fishing port called Angostura ('the Narrows') because it faces the first narrows in the Strait of Magellan. The houses are inhabited only in the short southern summer. Then, during the brief autumn and the long winter, they are no more than a point of reference in the landscape.

Angostura does not have a cemetery, but it does have a small, white-painted grave facing the sea. There lies Panchito Barría, a child who died at the age of eleven. People live and die everywhere – 'dying is a habit they tend to have', as the tango says – but Panchito's case is specially tragic, because he died of sadness.

Before reaching the age of three, Panchito suffered from

an attack of polio that left him crippled. His parents, fisher folk from San Gregorio in Patagonia, crossed the strait every summer to take up residence in Angostura. The child travelled with them: a precious bundle, propped up with blankets, watching the sea.

Until the age of five, Panchito Barría was a sad, shy child who hardly knew how to speak. But one fine day there occurred one of those miracles that are not unusual in the far south: a school of twenty or more southern dolphins appeared off Angostura, migrating from the Atlantic to the Pacific.

The locals who told me Panchito's story assured me that as soon as he saw them he let out a heart-rending cry, and as the dolphins went away his cries became louder and more disconsolate. Finally, just as the dolphins disappeared, from the child's throat came a shrill scream – a very high-pitched note that alarmed the fishermen and scared away the cormorants, but brought back one of the dolphins.

The dolphin came in close and began to jump out of the water. Panchito encouraged it with the shrill cries issuing from his throat. Everyone understood that a channel of communication had been opened between the dolphin and the child. There was no need for further explanation; it was just one of those things that happen in life. And that was that.

121

The dolphin stayed in the waters off Angostura all that summer. And as winter approached, obliging them to move north again, Panchito's parents and the other fishermen were astonished to observe that the child showed not the slightest sign of sorrow. With a gravity beyond his five years, he declared that his friend the dolphin also had to leave, otherwise he would be caught in the ice, but that he would come back the following year.

And the dolphin came back.

Panchito changed. He became a talkative, happy child, even making jokes about his crippled state. He changed radically. His games with the dolphin went on for seven years. Panchito learned to read and write, to draw his friend the dolphin. Like the other children, he helped to repair the nets, prepare ballast and dry shellfish, with his friend the dolphin playing offshore all the while, putting on a show just for him.

One morning in 1990 the dolphin didn't show up as usual. The fishermen were worried and searched for it, combing the strait from one end to the other. They didn't find it, but they did come across a Russian factory boat, one of the ocean's killers, very close to the strait's second narrows.

Two months later Panchito Barría died of sadness. He let his life seep away without crying or uttering a complaint.

I visited his grave, and from it I looked at the sea: the grey, choppy sea of incipient winter. The sea in which, until recently, dolphins played.

Chapter Seven

THE MAN facing me, who passes the maté gourd and then stirs the embers in the hearth, is called Carlos, and he is my oldest and best friend. He has a surname too, but he has asked me not to mention it if I write about what he is going to tell me this rainy day.

"Just Carlos," he insists, cutting some slices of horse-meat *charqui* – a snack that goes splendidly with maté.

"Alright. Just Carlos," I reply, listening to the rain getting heavier on the roof of the hangar that shelters us.

From a very early age, Just Carlos was only interested in one thing in life: flying. He read comics about airmen, his heroes were Malraux, Saint-Exupéry and Von Richtofen, the Red Baron. He only went to the cinema to see films about airmen, he collected model airplanes and at fifteen he could name all the parts of a real plane.

One afternoon on the beach in Valparaíso, when he was seventeen, he opened his heart to his family.

"I'm going to be a pilot. I have enrolled in the School of Aviation."

"That means you'll be in the military, you idiot. The School of Aviation belongs to the air force, in case you didn't know," they replied with brotherly affection.

"I know, but I have a plan for getting around that."

"Really? And may we know just what kind of trouble you are planning to get yourself into?"

"It's very simple. As soon as I learn how to fly a plane, I'll desert."

He learnt to fly light planes and helicopters, but he didn't have to desert. When the dictatorship began in 1973, Just Carlos was expelled from the air force for his socialist ideas.

When Chileans want to express a profound wellbeing, they say: "I'm happier than a dog with fleas." Just Carlos said: "I'm happier than a condor with fleas."

And where would an out-of-work pilot try his luck? In the far south, naturally. Just Carlos set out for Patagonia. He knew there were several pilots who did mail runs in that region neglected by the central bureaucracy. He arrived in Aisén, and within a few weeks met an airman who was something of a legend thereabouts: Captain Esquella, who flew supplies to the ranches of Patagonia and Tierra del Fuego in his DC-3.

His first job was as maintenance mechanic for *The Parrot with Hiccups*, the plane which no-one but Esquella flew until something happened that put Just Carlos into the pilot's seat.

"Esquella. Now there was a pilot!" exclaims Just Carlos, offering me a fresh maté.

In May 1975, Esquella had to make an emergency landing on a little beach on the Tres Montes Peninsula, facing the Golfo de Penas. The DC-3 was loaded with fine-wool sheep, and the flight from Puerto Montt went smoothly until one of the motors stopped and the plane began to lose altitude. His offsider suggested jettisoning the cargo: that is, throwing the sheep into the sea to lighten the plane, so as to maintain altitude and try to get to a landing strip on the mainland. Esquella refused. He made it clear that nobody was going to touch the cargo in his plane, and he looked for a beach.

It was not the most elegant of touchdowns. Part of the landing gear came off on the left-hand side, and the plane finally came to rest with its nose in the sea. But none of the sheep were harmed and, luckily, neither was the radio. Having received the SOS signal, Just Carlos set out in a boat to rescue the sheep and see what could be done with the DC-3.

Once the sheep were on board the boat, they checked over the plane. The fault in the motor could be easily fixed, and, apart from the damaged landing gear, *The Parrot with Hiccups* had come through pretty much unscathed. The plane could be repaired; the real problem was how to get it out of there.

"If you ask me, *The Parrot with Hiccups* has had it," remarked someone on the boat.

"Shut it, jerk. Are we going to get it out, Carlitos?" asked Esquella.

"Of course we're going to get it out," replied Just Carlos.

The guy who had declared *The Parrot with Hiccups* definitively earthbound was a fur trader with a notorious passion for gambling, and he couldn't pass up this opportunity.

"Esquella, I bet you five thousand pesos you can't get it out."

"Ten thousand says I can," replied the airman.

"Twenty thousand says no," insisted the trader.

"I bet fifty thousand I can get it out, flying," roared Esquella.

"OK. Fifty grand. Put it there."

They sealed the bet with a hearty handshake. Fifty

thousand new pesos. To Just Carlos it was a fortune. Esquella invited him to climb into the plane.

"Carlitos, fifty grand is at stake here. If we get it out, we'll go halves. Have you got any ideas?"

"Yes, but first I want to know how the weather's shaping up."

They asked for the weather report over the radio: for the next seventy-two hours the winds would be moderate.

"Tell the skipper of the boat that as soon as he's unloaded the sheep in Puerto Chacabuco, he's to hire two pairs of bullocks and buy or steal one of the catamarans from the yacht club. He's got to get back with all this within forty-eight hours."

The boat weighed anchor. Esquella, the offsider and Just Carlos set to work.

First they cut down several trees with flexible trunks and used them to prop up the plane. Then they cut other trunks from which they built a kind of path on which the plane's undercarriage could rest. Finally, they took the wheels off the undamaged landing gear and proceeded to lighten the plane by removing anything superfluous. When they were finished, after eighteen hours of work, there was nothing left inside *The Parrot with Hiccups* except the pilot's seat and the instruments.

The boat came back in time with everything they had

asked for. Plus the gambling trader, who kept telling them that he would spend part of the fifty thousand pesos, which he was sure he would win, treating them to a whole weekend at Coihaique's best brothel. The three men determined to get *The Parrot with Hiccups* airborne again just let him carry on.

The bullocks tugged at the plane until its nose came out of the water. They worked hard, those bullocks. A DC-3 weighs considerably more than a dray, but they were sturdy animals and they left it sitting straight on the tree-trunk path. Then the men detached the hulls from the catamaran and attached them to the plane in place of the landing gear. Finally, they tied a life raft to the fixed wheel at the rear to complete the conversion of *The Parrot with Hiccups* into a seaplane.

While the men from the boat went about making another two tree-trunk paths, one for each catamaran hull, Esquella and Just Carlos climbed into the plane and started up the engines. The DC-3's propellers spun perfectly.

"Now for the easy bit: taking off," said Esquella.

"You've got about three hundred metres of flat water. Then you come to the reefs," remarked Just Carlos.

"The problem will be landing. I've never flown a seaplane," Esquella confessed.

"The waters of the fiord will be calm. At least for the

next twenty-four hours. But listen, if you trust me, let me fly this wreck. At the School of Aviation I flew Grummans and Catalinas – they were lighter beasts than this, but I think I can do it."

"It's all yours, Carlitos. To make it lighter still we'll get rid of some of the fuel. You'll fly with just what you need. I'll be in the boat to give you the signal to take off."

"Let me have the seat then. I'm in charge here now."

"The fifty grand is yours, Carlitos."

The noble bullocks pulled *The Parrot with Hiccups* down into the water. The catamaran hulls supported the plane's weight, and the life raft kept the rear end afloat. Just Carlos waited till the boat got close to the line of the reefs before revving up the motors and getting the plane moving. It was a delight to see the needles of the tachometers oscillate. When he saw Esquella raise both thumbs, he pulled on the joystick and *The Parrot with Hiccups* took off, rapidly attaining the desired altitude.

It was a good flight, but bumpy despite the calm conditions, because the plane was so light that the breezes buffeted it like a sheet of paper. Without a hitch, he flew one hundred and forty-five kilometres north over the Taitao Peninsula and the San Rafael glacier, to the mouth of the great fiord of Aisén. There he turned east and, guided by the flashing water, headed inland. He still had twelve kilometres to go to the bay of Puerto Chacabuco when the needle on the fuel gauge fell to empty. But he was safe by then and, with the help of the breezes from the Pacific, he glided the rest of the way without a problem. He landed on the water like a swan, to the noisy delight of the locals gathered on the pier.

The fur trader paid up. With the fifty thousand pesos, Carlos decided to start his own business. He soon met Pet Manheim, another pilot in search of open skies, and together they set up the region's first itinerant fruit and vegetable market: Blossoming Enterprise.

They started out with a Piper plane and a Sikorsky helicopter left over from the Korean War. In Puerto Montt they loaded the plane with onions, lettuces, tomatoes, apples, oranges and other fruit and vegetables, and flew them to Puerto Aisén, where they had their base; from there they went out in the helicopter to supply the villages and ranches of Patagonia.

Blossoming Enterprise lasted until the unlucky day when Pet and the helicopter disappeared, caught in an unforeseen storm. No sign of them was ever found. They lie somewhere among the glaciers, forests and lakes of Patagonia, which attract and sometimes swallow up adventurers.

Having lost his partner and the helicopter, Just Carlos

changed his line of business and started running a postal service between Patagonia and Tierra del Fuego. But, things happening the way they do in Patagonia, one day he found himself piloting the first aerial hearse in the southern skies.

One June morning, deep in winter, Just Carlos was in the stockyards of a ranch near Ushuaia. He was checking over the Piper before flying back north, and waiting for the gauchos to finish roasting a lamb. Suddenly a Land Rover appeared and four strangers climbed out of it.

"Who's the pilot of the Piper?" asked one.

"Me. What's up?"

"You have to do us a favour. You'll be paid whatever you ask," said the man.

"Whatever you ask. Money is no problem," put in another of the strangers.

"Calm down. What's all this about?"

"Don Nicanor Estrada, the owner of the San Benito ranch, has died. I am the overseer," declared the man in charge.

"My sincere condolences. And what does this have to do with me?"

"You have to take him to Comodoro Rivadavia. His family is waiting for him there, ready for the wake. Don Nicanor must be buried in the family tomb."

They didn't know what they were talking about. The San Benito ranch is in Río Grande, eight hundred kilometres from Comodoro Rivadavia, and that's as the crow flies.

"Sorry. My plane doesn't have that sort of range. I have just enough fuel to get to Punta Arenas," said Just Carlos by way of an excuse.

"You'll take him. Didn't you hear who it is?" insisted the overseer.

"No. I'm not taking him. And just to spell things out: *I* decide when and where I fly, and who I take as passengers."

"You don't understand. If you refuse to take Don Nicanor Estrada, you're not going to fly again in Patagonia, Tierra del Fuego or any other damned part of the world."

Even before the overseer had finished speaking, his companions lifted up their ponchos to reveal sawn-off shotguns.

Sometimes it is best to make exceptions. So thought Just Carlos as he flew towards the San Benito ranch with a thug in the co-pilot's seat.

Don Nicanor was waiting for him, blue and frozen, in the funeral chapel they had set up in the ranch's cold-storage room. Hundreds of skinned lambs kept the boss company. A few gauchos and farmhands were drinking maté and smoking, between fearful glances at the dead body.

"He's huge," said Carlos.

"Like all the Estradas. A metre ninety-seven," said the overseer.

"It won't fit. A package that big won't fit in the Piper," Just Carlos pointed out.

"Have some respect for Don Nicanor. He will fit," insisted the overseer.

"Listen, I understand that you have to do everything possible to get the stiff to Comodoro Rivadavia. But *you* have to understand that it's impossible. This plane is a Piper, a four-seater. From the instrument panel to the back corner of the cabin is only a metre and seventy centimetres. He won't even fit in diagonally."

"What about putting him in lying down or sitting. That way he'll fit."

"That won't work either. The back seat is ninety centimetres across. So lying down is no good, and as for sitting, how long has he been dead?"

"Four days, why?"

"Four days! He'll be stiff as a plank, because he's frozen, but also because of rigor mortis. You'd have to break his spine, and I don't think the family would like that."

"Shit no," agreed the overseer.

The dead man, as well as being tall, was very solidly built. He must have weighed a good hundred and twenty kilos without clothes, but stretched out there in all his get-up – silver spurs, high boots, *chiripá*, broad leather belt trimmed with silver, gaucho knife and poncho – he would have been over a hundred and fifty.

"Listen, can you take off part of the roof?" asked the overseer.

"I can take it all off. But then I freeze."

"Just part of it. Enough to fit the body in. You can fly at low altitude."

"You're crazy. You want me to take it standing up?"

"I don't care how, but you're taking it, you son of a bitch," yelled the overseer, squashing Carlos's nose with the barrel of a .38.

He took it. After removing the co-pilot's door and tying the body to a plank, they put it into the Piper feet first. They tied the feet firmly to the bottom of the back seat, the dead man's waist resting against the back of the co-pilot's seat, and part of his torso, his shoulders and head poking out the top of the plane. Since they put him in facing upwards, he seemed to be looking at the right wing. To finish off the job, they covered his head with a plastic bag on which was written 'San Benito. The Best Meat'.

Before taking off, Just Carlos reflected that flying an aerial hearse wasn't a bad lurk. The overseer had given him a cheque for fifty thousand Chilean pesos and the other half of his fee was waiting for him in Comodoro Rivadavia.

He looked at the fuel gauge: full. The farmhands had found enough fuel for the first leg, which would take him to Río Gallegos. Three hundred and fifty kilometres flying at low altitude, bundled up like an Eskimo, with a passenger half in, half out.

He took off at two in the afternoon. Luckily the weather was good, but the strong winds from the Atlantic made the Piper bounce around like a cocktail shaker. After flying for forty-five minutes, Cape Espíritu Santo came into sight and he crossed the Strait of Magellan. He was singing at the top of his voice. When he had exhausted his repertoire of tangos, cumbias and boleros, he moved on to the national anthem and hymns from school he could hardly remember. He had to sing at the top of his voice to keep his body warm.

At five it was already dark and he could hardly make out the line of foam along the Atlantic coast. When he requested authorisation to land on the strip at Río Gallegos, they asked if he had any cargo to declare.

"I'm not carrying cargo. I'm carrying a dead body. Over."

"Have you got the medical certificate indicating the cause of death? Over."

"No. No-one told me anything about that. Over."

"Well, go back and get it. Over."

"The stiff is called Nicanor Estrada. Over."

A powerful man, Don Nicanor, influential even as a corpse. The priest who was waiting for him on the airstrip almost had a heart attack when he saw the uncomfortable position the passenger had travelled in.

"He can't stay in there. God forbid! You must get him out and take him straight to the cathedral," cried the priest.

"No way. He's staying here. In the fresh air," said Just Carlos.

"What kind of vermin are you? This is Don Nicanor Estrada!" bellowed the priest.

"If you take him to the church, he'll thaw out and start to rot. I imagine that the family wants to receive Don Nicanor's body uncorrupted."

After being excommunicated, Just Carlos talked the priest round to a compromise: a Mass, OK, but right there, with the body in the plane. So Don Nicanor Estrada was treated to a religious service on the airstrip, at ten degrees below zero.

That night, Just Carlos slept like a log under the blankets off three beds, in a boarding house near the airstrip. The next day, at six in the morning, he downed a litre of coffee, armed himself with two thermos flasks full of the steaming beverage, and took off at first light on the second leg of the flight: from Río Gallegos to Río Chico, over the Atlantic and Bahía Grande, until the lighthouse of Cape San Francisco de Paula came into view, marking the beginning of the overland section. The two-hundred-kilometre flight went smoothly, helped along by the Georges Moustaki songs which the need to keep warm fetched out of Just Carlos's memory for him to howl at the top of his voice between one bolero and the next.

At ten in the morning, after refuelling in Río Chico, he set off on the third leg of the funerary tour to Las Martinetas, a village another two hundred kilometres on, quite a way from the coast. He flew along the line of the road that leads to Comodoro Rivadavia. Beneath him rushed the pampa, flocks of sheep and groups of rheas, which from that height looked like grotesque chicks with their bottoms in the air. The rheas fled in fright at the noise of the Piper.

At two in the afternoon, Just Carlos and Don Nicanor Estrada began the last leg of the journey. Another two hundred kilometres and they would be in Comodoro Rivadavia. There was not a cloud in the sky, the dead man's frozen hood glistened in the sun, and Just Carlos went on singing, hoarsely now, promising himself that the first thing he would do when he got back to Chile would be to take singing lessons.

When he requested permission to use the airstrip at

Comodoro Rivadavia, they asked him why he was flying at such a low altitude. The radar of the Argentinian Air Force had only just detected him.

"It's because I have a dead man on board. A famous dead man. Over."

"Who the hell are you? Over."

"Southern Air Hearses. Over," replied Just Carlos with the pitiful remains of his voice.

On the airstrip, the family of the dead man and the local authorities welcomed him with fainting, insults and threats, which, as they listened to his explanation, modulated into hollow phrases of apology.

As he was still waiting for his second cheque, Just Carlos had no choice but to join the funeral procession. A surprise was waiting for him at the cemetery. After a solemn Mass, the cortege headed for the family tomb, which was like a little palace of white marble. Having removed the dead man from the casket with the help of a crane, they lifted him up by the armpits, put a gaucho hat on his head and finally lowered him into an enormous pit. Just Carlos looked over the edge. Down in the pit was an embalmed horse. Don Nicanor Estrada was buried on horseback.

"Then what happened?" I ask, as the storm intensifies.

"I got paid, paid off my debts and came back. You stir up the fire, I'm going to get a piece of meat to put in the coals," says Just Carlos, moving off lazily.

He is my oldest and best friend. Often, when I am far away from the South, I worry that something awful may have happened to him. And now the dents in the fuselage of the Piper make me worry too.

Just Carlos comes back with a rack of lamb.

"What are you going to do, Carlitos."

"I'm going to roast it."

"No. I mean later, tomorrow, whenever."

"Fly. As soon as the weather improves I'll take you for a spin around the Golfo Elefantes. You came to see whales. Well, you'll see them," says Just Carlos, throwing sprigs of rosemary onto the meat, his child-like eyes observing the fire for a while, then me, then the plane, which is enjoying the warmth of the hangar like a third companion, sheltered from the rain that goes on falling over Patagonia.

Chapter Eight

THE ARRIVAL of winter surprises me in Puerto Natales. Just forty-eight hours ago I was strolling on the beach by the Golfo Almirante Montt, admiring the sunset at the close of a glorious April day. But yesterday it began to snow heavily, and the temperature plummeted from six degrees to minus four. The radio tells me the airport has been closed. So getting out of here has become particularly difficult.

Puerto Natales is on the east side of the Golfo Almirante Montt. To the west lie two hundred and fifty kilometres of labyrinthine canals leading to the Nelson Strait and the Pacific. Only the seamen of Chiloé venture into those narrow passageways where a freezing death may await them; blocks of ice detached from the glaciers by the tides often stop the canals for months.

It is impossible to get out of Puerto Natales by sea in winter. You have to go overland, across the border to El Turbio, in Argentina. That is where the world's southern-most railway starts, the line of the original *Patagonia Express*, which after covering two hundred and forty kilometres and linking up towns like El Zurdo and Bella-vista, arrives at Río Gallegos on the Atlantic coast.

The train, made up of two passenger carriages and two goods vans, is drawn by an old coal-fired locomotive made in Japan at the beginning of the thirties. Two long wooden benches run the length of each passenger carriage. At one end is a wood stove which the passengers have to stoke for themselves, and, above it, a coloured print of the Virgin of Luján.

There are not many passengers with me in the train. Just a pair of farmhands who started snoring as soon as they collapsed onto the benches, and a Protestant minister bent over double trying to study the New Testament with his nose between the pages. I feel like offering him my glasses.

"There's wood there. Make sure the stove doesn't go out," the ticket inspector advises me.

"Thanks. I don't have a ticket. I tried to buy one in El Turbio but they didn't have any."

"Don't worry. Buy it at the next stop, Jaramillo."

A layer of snow covers the pastures, and the pampa's perpetual green-brown motley takes on a spectral hue. The *Patagonia Express* advances into a monotonous white landscape, which puts the minister to sleep. The Bible falls from his hands and closes. It looks like a black brick.

The *Patagonia Express* really belongs to the men who work the sheep. At the end of every winter, hundreds of men from Chiloé arrive in Puerto Natales, cross the border and take the train to the sheep farms. They're hardy types, sick of the poor life on Chiloé and the proverbial harshness of the island women, and they come to the mainland to make their fortune. They're hardy, but they die young. On Chiloé they live on seafood and potatoes; in Patagonia, on lamb and potatoes. Very few have ever tasted fruit – except apples – or green vegetables. Stomach cancer is endemic among them.

The Jaramillo station is a wooden building painted red. There is something vaguely Scandinavian about its architecture. The intricate tiles that decorate the guttering swing in the wind. Many are missing and those that remain will fall without a hand being lifted to attach them firmly or put them back.

There is nothing much in Jaramillo besides the station and a pair of houses, but the train stops there to take on water. That seems to be the place's main function, though it also keeps alive the memory of a Patagonian tragedy, a memory to which the hands of the station clock, stopped at nine twenty-eight, bear persistent witness.

In 1921 the last major revolt of farmhands and Indians broke out on the La Anita ranch. Four thousand men and women, led by a Galician anarchist called Antonio Soto, took over the ranch and the station. They proclaimed the right to self-government, and for a couple of weeks lived under the illusion of having created Patagonia's first Free Commune or Soviet, as they ingenuously christened it. The reaction of the landholders was not long in coming. The Argentinian government sent a strong military contingent to put down the insurrection. The soldiers arrived at midday on the eighteenth day of June 1921.

The men of the commune took up positions in the Jaramillo station while the women stayed on at the ranch, occupying the houses. They were armed with gaucho knives, a pair of revolvers snatched from the overseers, spears and *boleadoras*. The army had rifles and machine guns.

After having surrounded the station, Captain Varela, who was in charge of the troops, gave the insurgents until ten at night to give themselves up, promising not to kill any of those who laid down their arms. But a soldier's word being what it is, he didn't wait that long, and at nine twenty-eight he gave the order to open fire.

Just how many died has never been established. Hundreds of men were shot beside graves they had been forced to dig themselves. Hundreds of bodies were burnt, and the smell of the charred corpses spread over the pampa.

Nine twenty-eight. A bullet stopped the clock, and that is how it stays.

"It's been repaired lots of times, but somebody always stops it again and sets the hands to that time," the ticket inspector informs me.

"They were all subversives. That Galician, their leader, he convinced them that property was theft. It was a good thing that they were all killed. You have to be merciless with subversives," says the minister, butting in.

The farmhands, who have woken up, reply with obscene gestures; the ticket inspector shrugs his shoulders and the minister takes refuge in the scrutiny of his black brick.

The sun is going down in the west, sinking into the Pacific, and its last rays project the shadow of the *Patagonia Express* onto the white pampa as the train moves in the opposite direction, towards the Atlantic, where the days begin.

Chapter Nine

I ALWAYS come back to Río Mayo, a Patagonian town about a hundred kilometres from Coihaique and two hundred kilometres from Comodoro Rivadavia. I always come back, and the first thing I do when I get off the bus, truck or whatever vehicle drops me at the crossroads is shut my eyes so as not to be blinded by the dust. Then I open them slowly, shoulder my pack, and walk towards an elaborately carved wooden building.

It is a noble ruin, a mute witness to better times. Given a shove, the door opens to reveal what remains of the orchestra podium, the bar – its stools covered with brown leather, now mostly eaten by goats – and the portrait of Queen Victoria painted on the wall of the reception hall by somebody with a highly personal understanding of anatomy. The eyes of the British sovereign have slid sideways and almost touch her ears, while her flared nostrils, distinctly African in form, occupy half of her face.

"*Salve, Regina*," I say in greeting, and sit myself down to smoke a cigarette before bidding her goodbye. I know for sure that one of the locals will be waiting for me outside. This time it's a woman. Gripping a basket, she watches me with mischievous eyes.

"You're in the wrong place," she says.

"Isn't this the Hotel Inglés?"

"Yes, but it's been shut for ten years, since the gringo died."

"What? When did Mister Simpson die?" I ask, though I already know the story, just for the pleasure of hearing a new version.

"Ten years ago. He shut himself up with five women, you know, women on the game. And he died, the dirty old man."

Five women. The last time I was here, a local told me it was twelve French prostitutes. Perhaps legends dwindle. In any case, what is certain is that when Thomas Simpson found out that cancer was gnawing at his bones and the doctor gave him three months at the most to live, he gave the hotel to his employees and kept only the Presidential Suite for himself. He had some boxes of Havana cigars and

147

a barrel of Scotch sent up to the suite, and he shut himself in with an undetermined number of lively, well-paid ladies, whose task was to hasten his death in the most pleasurable manner.

Within a week, the news of his sweet agony had reached Comodoro Rivadavia. The English community got together and sent a clergyman to put a stop to the scandal, but when the bearer of good news tried to get into the suite, he was stopped by a .45-calibre piece of lead which ripped through one of his legs. Simpson died as he wished to die, and the hotel went to the dogs in no time at all.

"There's another hotel at the end of the street. If you like, I'll take you there," says the woman.

I decline her offer, but set off in the direction she has indicated. I know where I'm headed: the Hotel San Martín, Patagonia's best.

It is a big, rambling, one-storey building on a corner. Through the clouds of dust that are always blowing down the street, I see that there is a man at the top of a ladder repainting the sign that identifies the establishment.

"Excuse me. Are you the owner of the hotel?" I call out from below.

"If I was the owner, I wouldn't be up here," he yells from above.

"Can you get the owner?"

"He's not here. No-one is. Go in and have some maté," yells the painter.

I do as he says, and as I push open the double doors it occurs to me that he's not an Argentinian, that guy. There's too much of a lilt in his accent.

The dining room hasn't changed over the last few years. The same iron tables with formica tops, the same wooden chairs, and on each table, a coquettish vase with plastic roses and carnations. Bottles of wine, grappa and *caña* are lined up behind the wooden bar. And in the place of honour, on the mirror, is a portrait of tango legend Carlos Gardel displaying perfect teeth.

The Hotel San Martín. Until 1978 the place was used as the municipal wine cellar. That year, two political 'offenders' were relegated to Río Mayo: Gerardo Garib the Turk, who wasn't a Turk at all, but an Argentinian from Buenos Aires, a unionist untainted by Peronism and descended from Palestinians; and Susana Grimaldi, also known as the Turk, though there was nothing Turkish about her either – except of course that she was married to Gerardo – since she was a Uruguayan from Colonia, a music teacher, who could swear superbly in the Italian of her forebears.

Susana and Gerardo were lucky during the dictatorship. They were subjected to the monstrous experience of the military prisons and the disappearances, they were tortured, but they emerged from the labyrinth of horror alive, condemned to five years of internal exile in Patagonia.

They were both enterprising people: a year and a half after arriving, Susana was giving music lessons to a dozen aspiring Gardels, and Gerardo had managed to rent premises for a hotel.

"Did you help yourself to maté?" asks the painter, coming in and interrupting my thoughts.

"No. I was just about to."

"Are you hungry? I can make you some pancakes if you like. I make the best pancakes in Patagonia. They're famous, my pancakes."

"Are you Chilean?"

"From Chiloé. I came to work on a ranch, but I got sick and the Turk took me on as cook, barman and renovator."

"Where is the Turk? And Susana?"

"So you know them. They went to the funeral."

"What funeral? Whose funeral?"

"An old guy. Carlitos, he was called."

"Carlitos Carpintero?"

"That's the one. You knew him too?"

Carlitos Carpintero. In 1988, in Stockholm, the organisation that awards the alternative Nobel prizes decided to honour a mysterious professor called Klaus

Kucimavic with the alternative Nobel prize for physics. In 1980, this Professor Kucimavic had written long letters to several European universities explaining that, according to his observations in Patagonia, a dangerous hole was opening up in the layer of ozone that shields the atmosphere. The accuracy of his figures for the diameter of the hole and the rate of its expansion was confirmed eight years later by NASA and several European scientific institutions. Professor Kucimavic could not be summoned to accept his prize because no-one knew how to get in touch with him. All that was written on the back of his letters was: Province of Chubut, Argentina.

A German periodical hired me to travel to Patagonia to find the mysterious professor. I visited several villages and towns without success, and eventually ended up in Río Mayo. I made friends with Gerardo and Susana, and one night they invited me to a *truco* competition organised by Carlos Alberto Valente, one of the most eccentric and admirable gauchos I have met. We played and laughed until the small hours, and then, over supper, as we were talking about what we did, I told Valente why I was in Río Mayo.

"What did you say his name was again?"

"Kucimavic. Klaus Kucimavic."

"Carlos Carpintero. That's what he's called: Carlos Carpintero."

"Who's Carlos Carpintero?"

"The person you're looking for. A crazy old guy who turned up here years and years ago. Crazy, but not stupid. He invents things. For example, he invented a system for me which converts cow manure into gas. I have free hot water. The old guy calls it biogas. Crazy for sure, but no fool. He spends a lot of time looking at the sky and measuring the sun's rays with mirrors. He says that in a few years we'll all go blind."

The next day I met Kucimavic. He was a skinny old man, enveloped in greasy mechanic's overalls. When I came to see him he was repairing or improving a shower system for dipping sheep.

He denied straight away that he was called Klaus Kucimavic, and in his distinctive Spanish he swore that he was Argentinian born and bred.

"If you're Argentinian, how come you talk gibberish?" asked Valente.

"I speak the Spanish better than you, you ugly ass," replied the old man.

But he had once entrusted to Valente a document issued by the Argentinian authorities which identified him as Kucimavic. When he saw it was useless to go on pretending, he agreed to talk, reluctantly.

He was born in Slovenia. During the Second World War

he joined the ranks of the Croatian Ustashi, fighting along-side the Nazis in the Balkans. At the end of the war he managed to avoid being tried by Tito's partisans and emigrated to Argentina, determined to start a new life in South America. But he soon found that the Israelis, encouraged by the capture of Adolf Eichmann, were stepping up the search for ex-Nazis and collaborators in Argentina. So Klaus Kucimavic gave up his chair in physics at the University of Buenos Aires and disappeared into Patagonia, a part of the world where no questions are asked and the past is a strictly personal matter.

Everyone liked him in Río Mayo. He was an obliging old guy who, despite his reputation for being unsociable, would not hesitate to repair a radio, an iron, a tap or a motor, without charging a cent.

He admitted that the measurements of the ozone layer were his and stubbornly refused to talk about the prize.

"You tell those jerks they should be putting a stop to atmospheric pollution instead of handing out prizes. Prizes are for beauty queens," he said angrily.

I had collected enough raw material for a long article on the man who had discovered the hole in the ozone layer, but if I had published it I would have upset the harmony of Río Mayo; so I put it aside, and for me too, Kucimavic became Carlos Carpintero.

"Carlitos has left us," said Garib the Turk, hugging me.

"I knew you'd come back. Welcome," said Susana in greeting.

That afternoon we sat down to eat very early. I found out for myself that the man from Chiloé was indeed a good cook and that his pancakes were unbeatable. We talked about how things had turned out for us. I could have gone back to Chile, but I was staying on in Europe. They could have gone back to Buenos Aires, but were staying on in Patagonia. Talking to them convinced me once again that the place you feel best is where you belong.

"You know, the last time, when you left, I had the feeling that you were in a quandary. I guess it was hard for you not to write about Carlitos," said Susana, filling the glasses with grappa.

"Yes, it really weighed on my conscience. I couldn't stop wondering: what if Carlitos turned out to have been a war criminal, a fascist like the ones who screwed up our lives?"

"No, Carlitos was just a guy who fought on the wrong side. He wasn't a criminal," affirmed the Turk.

"How can you be so sure?"

"In Patagonia, you learn to judge what people are like from the way they look at you. Carlitos was myopic, that's why he wore those glasses like bottle-ends; but when he was talking to a friend, he took them off and looked you straight in the eyes. And his gaze was clear."

"Tell him about his last words," said Susana.

"His last words. Typical! He came out of the coma a couple of minutes before dying. He took my hand, and said: 'Ah shit, Gerardo. I didn't fix your fridge.' You see? If Carlitos had had something on his conscience, he wouldn't have been worrying about my fridge when he died."

Susana got up to serve some other patrons and opened the windows that gave onto the street. Outside, the wind had dropped, and with no dust in the air you could see the footpath on the other side of the road. There was nothing at that moment between the people and the calm Patagonian night.

Chapter Ten

"**L**EAVE THE bottle," I tell the boy who has just served me a glass of rum. I lift the glass to my lips. A vague solace spreads through me, alleviating my exhaustion and the torpor caused by the hot, humid air coming from the jungle.

I am in Shell, a town on the verge of the Amazon basin in Ecuador, sitting in a canteen without a door or windows. Outside I can see the unmoving fronds of the palm trees in the town's only street, heat-stunned too, under the cloudless sky.

A good sky for flying with Captain Palacios. I wonder what his first name is. For the locals, the aviator who used to dispose of his earthbound hours rocking in a hammock and putting away bottles of San Miguel rum was just

Captain Palacios. And that's how he was known in the hundreds of Amazonian villages and towns he visited in his clapped-out little plane. And his partner? What was his partner called?

I met them one afternoon when I was looking for a flight from Shell to San Sebastián del Coca. A truck dropped me off in what seemed to be a broad street. As soon as I stepped down I felt my feet sink into the mud, and I saw that I was not alone; several pigs were happily wallowing in the mire.

"How do I get to the airport," I asked the truck driver.

"Here it is, my friend. All this beside the road here is airport," he said, pointing to a wide field of mud.

On one side of the field was a wooden building with a galvanised-iron roof. I set off in that direction, and as I approached the building, I heard the voice of a sports commentator broadcasting a soccer match.

The building had sliding doors and they were open. Inside, a massive mulatto was looking at some metal parts sitting in half a drum of petrol. With one hand he moved them slowly, letting the petrol strip them of accumulated dirt; in the other hand he held a long cigar. The movements of his head suggested complete disagreement with what the commentator was saying. A green tarpaulin stretched from wall to wall divided the interior of the building, hiding the rear section. The mulatto looked at me with a total lack of

157

interest, then turned his attention once again to the soccer match.

"Good afternoon," I said in greeting.

"That's a matter of opinion. What can I do for you?"

"I have to fly to Coca. Can you tell me what I need to do?"

"Sure. To fly, you just have to flap your arms, run to get up a bit of speed and pull up your feet. Something else?"

"Cut the crap, will you. I have to fly to Coca."

"Sure. You need to talk to Captain Palacios."

"Where can I find him?"

"In Catalina's bar, naturally. Squelch through the mud to the end of the street. And careful with the pigs. They're real sons of bitches."

Catalina's bar was in a hut about thirty square metres in size. The bar itself was at the back, and there were a few men there, drinking and talking. In the middle hung a jute hammock, and in it was a man with grey hair, sleeping soundly. To one side, a man and a woman waited, with expressions of infinite patience, busy just keeping their rocking chairs rocking. The woman was holding a sack on her lap. From it emerged the heads of two very small pigs. The man's feet rested on a wire cage, from which a rooster with irate eyes glared hatefully at the piglets.

"I'm looking for Captain Palacios," I said to the woman

who was serving behind the bar.

"Right there, honey," she replied, pointing to the occupant of the hammock.

"Can I wake him up?"

"It depends what for. He goes wild if he's woken up for no good reason."

"I have to fly to Coca . . ."

That was all I got to say. The woman with the piglets got up as if moved by a spring and started to shake the hammock.

"Bloody hell, what's going on?" mumbled the man, emerging from sleep.

"You've got another passenger. That fills the plane up. Now we can fly," said the woman, still shaking the hammock.

Captain Palacios stretched, rubbed his eyes, yawned, and finally got out of the hammock. He was no more than a metre sixty tall, and he was wearing faded pilot's overalls, the kind with zips everywhere.

"What's the weather like?" he asked no-one in particular.

"Like shit," replied one of the men at the bar.

"It could be worse. OK, let's fly," retorted Palacios.

With a resolute gait, he left the bar. The woman with the piglets, the man with the rooster and I followed him. At the airport, the mulatto who had sent me to the bar was still busy cleaning the metal parts and listening to the soccer.

"Take their money, partner," Palacios told him as soon as we entered the building.

"What? You're going to fly in this weather?!" exclaimed the mulatto, pointing at the roof. Not much further up, grey clouds promised a storm.

"Vultures fly and they're uglier than me, so I don't see why I shouldn't," replied Palacios.

"Stubborn bastard. Alright, you lot, give me your names. It's handy to have them for identifying the bodies if there's an accident. Two hundred and fifty sucres per head," announced the mulatto.

The woman with the piglets was going to Mondaña, a little settlement about ninety kilometres from Shell, also accessible by other means – first on foot to Chontapunta, then by canoe on the Napo River – so long as the weather is good and you have the patience to undertake a two- or three-day journey.

The man with the rooster was going as far as San José de Payamino, a village on the Payamino River. San José de Payamino's cockfighting ring is famous in the Amazon. The stakes are high there, and often fortunes built up by prospectors over hard years of destroying the jungle and their own lives leak away with the blood of the defeated bird, and end up in the purses of the professional gamblers. The man was going to try his luck with his champion rooster. That little coppery bird was a killing machine. Or so said its owner, declaring that the week before it had ripped the guts out of eight opponents in the ring at Macas. He too could have travelled overland and by river, but it would have taken about five days and tired out the bird.

"What are you waiting for? It's hauling time!" cried Palacios, pulling back the green tarpaulin. There was the little plane. An old, discoloured four-seater Cessna.

With the other men, I pulled on the ropes tied to the landing gear and we dragged the old bomb out onto the strip. I looked at the very conspicuous mends in the fuse-lage and was on the point of repenting, but I had to get to Coca, a hundred and eighty kilometres away, and the quickest way was by air.

Repeating to myself, like a prayer, "These planes are safe, very safe, absolutely safe," I climbed aboard. I got the co-pilot's seat. The piglets grunted nervously behind me, but the rooster paid no attention to the busy preparation for take-off.

"San Sebastián . . . San Sebastián . . . do you read me . . .?"

Captain Palacios was talking into a microphone. All he got by way of a reply was a series of whistles. After twiddling some knobs, which only made the whistles

161

louder, he hung up the microphone.

"I told you to fix this thing. I told you."

"It's buggered, that thing. I'm a mechanic, not a miracle-worker," said the mulatto.

"Alright. What the hell. They'll see us coming anyway."

As the plane began to bump along over the mud, I looked at the instrument panel and felt a sudden desire to jump out. Never before had I seen such a humble panel. Among the empty sockets and the cable-ends that were once, no doubt, connected to navigation instruments, two needles could be seen oscillating: those of the altimeter and the fuel gauge. The artificial horizon, which should be parallel to the land surface, was practically vertical.

"Hey, the horizon isn't working," I said, hiding my panic.

"It doesn't matter. The sky's above and the land's below. The rest is all bullshit," said Palacios, definitively.

We took off. The plane climbed to about one hundred and fifty metres and stabilised smoothly. We were flying under a ceiling of thick, grey clouds. The warm air of an imminent storm occupied the cabin. It was some relief to see that the compass was working: we were heading north-east. After twenty minutes we saw the winding green line of a river.

"Isn't it beautiful: the Huapuno. We're in the Amazon already!" exclaimed the pilot.

"I thought the Amazon started a fair bit further east," I remarked.

"Politicians' bullshit. The Amazon begins with the first drops that end up in the big river. What did you leave behind in Coca?"

"Nothing. I'm visiting some friends."

"That's good. You should never forget your friends. Even if they are in hell itself, you should go and see them. I thought you were a prospector. I don't like prospectors."

"Neither do I."

"They're a plague. At the slightest rumour of a bit of shiny shit they appear in their thousands. Sometimes I feel like loading up the plane with poison gas and fumigating them. How are you enjoying the flight?"

"Good so far. No complaints."

Captain Palacios's flight plan was fairly simple: staying under the clouds, he followed the Huapuno River until it joined the Arajuno to form a bigger river flowing northwest. Below, the jungle was like a gigantic animal at rest, waiting, resigned, for the downpour that would not be long in coming.

"You're not from round here, are you?"

"No. I'm Chilean."

"Ah, that's good."

"Why do you say that?"

"Well, either you're here because you're crazy or because you can't stay in your country, and either of those reasons is just fine by me. Look at the flamingos down there. Have you ever seen more beautiful birds?"

He was right about everything: you had to be crazy to get into that plane, it was true that I couldn't stay in my country, and down below, in a lagoon formed by the overflow of the Huapuno, there was a crowd of beautiful flamingos waiting for the storm.

After flying for an hour, we spotted a clearing in the jungle, clinging to the west bank of the Napo. In the clearing were four or five houses built of reeds and palm fronds. That was Mondaña. After dropping about fifty metres, we began to circle.

"Don't worry. It's just to give the boys time to clear the strip."

Below, several figures ran to the beach, removed branches and stones, and then, waving their arms, gave us the all clear. Palacios demonstrated that he could land on a handkerchief.

After dropping off the woman and her piglets, and being charged with several errands by the locals, we prepared for the second take-off. Palacios moved the craft to one end of the beach, sped up, and took off practically level with the water. Within a few minutes we were following the course of the Napo.

"You still nervous there?" asked Palacios, ironically.

"Not as much as at the start. Have you been flying long? That was a fantastic take-off from the beach back there."

"Maybe, but I was shitting myself," said the man with the rooster from behind.

"Too long. I don't even know how long any more," replied Captain Palacios.

"Do you own the plane?"

"You could say we own each other. Without it, I wouldn't know what to do, and without me, it wouldn't go anywhere. Look how beautiful the Napo is. Twice a year this section of it floods over big areas of jungle and they catch enormous catfish."

"Sure do. Not long ago I saw them catch one that weighed over sixty kilos," said the man with the rooster.

"Why are you interested in the plane? Do you know about planes?"

"A bit. The motor sounds good."

"For sure. I have a good mechanic. The mulatto you saw in Shell is my partner, and he makes sure that everything is running well. This plane belonged to some priests who had to make a crash-landing near Macas. They landed in the treetops and left it there. We bought it as scrap metal and in a couple of months we had it flying again."

The landing strip at San José de Payamino was a broad

165

open space, cleared by hand with machetes. It was also used as a soccer oval, market place and town square. There we left the man with the rooster, wished him luck, refuelled and continued our journey, flying along the Payamino River until its waters joined those of the Puno. Later, still heading north-west, flying over San Francisco de Orellana, we saw the Puno and the Coca flow into the great Napo River, which turns towards the south-east. Its waters have to travel over a thousand kilometres before they feed into the magnificent, powerful current of the Amazon.

During the last leg of the flight, the aviator told me a bit about his life. He had been a pilot with Texaco, on a very high salary, until one day he realised that he didn't like gringos and that he'd fallen in love with the Amazon.

"It's like a woman. It gets right into you, under your skin. It asks for nothing, but you end up doing everything you think it wants."

We went on talking in San Sebastián del Coca, and after a night on the town, during which we filled ourselves up to the ears with rum, we decided that we could be friends. And what a friend he was. He showed me, from the air, the most secret and fascinating regions of the Amazon, and many of the mysteries of that green world, which he knew better than he knew himself.

Several years after our first flight, when I came back to

do a series of reports on the criminal destruction of the jungle, Captain Palacios was there, ready to take me wherever I needed to go. The last time I saw him was in the Pantanal, between Brazil and Paraguay, in the lower Mato Grosso. We took leave of each other euphorically, our spirits lifted by the rum drunk in a ritual of friendship and the satisfaction of having done a good job shooting a documentary on the extermination of the *jacarés*, Amazonian crocodiles whose skins end up on show in European fashion parades. All of the crew who worked on the documentary agreed that it would have been an impossible task without the help of Captain Palacios.

"Be seeing you. I don't need to tell you to come back. The Amazon has got under your skin too, and you can't live without it. Whenever you want to have a go at the bastards who are destroying it, you know where you can find me."

And I looked for him. Before sitting down in this canteen and ordering the bottle of rum I am gradually emptying, I wore myself out looking for him. I couldn't find him, or his partner, the mulatto. Somebody told me that they had taken off together for an unknown destination and not come back. This person didn't remember exactly when. Lives are swallowed up by oblivion too quickly in this part of the world.

What has become of those two magnificent adventurers? What happened to that man whose first name I never knew, and who never used mine? My friend, Captain Palacios.

Final Part

Note on Arrival

SOMEBODY TAPPED me on the shoulder.

"Wake up. We're in Martos."

It took me a while to recognise the driver and realise that I was in a bus. Less than an hour ago I had caught it in Jaén, and as soon as my head came to rest on the back of the seat, I had fallen into a deep sleep.

"Martos?"

"That's where we are."

As soon as I got off the bus, I felt the midday sun beating down like a club. There was not a single cloud in the sky and not the slightest breeze stirring. The streets displayed the immaculate whiteness of their houses, adorned with green shutters, and scattered all about were pots containing the plants I like best: humble, hardy geraniums.

There was no-one in the streets, but I knew this was normal in southern Spain during the hottest part of the day. The sound of a radio came from one of the houses, and making my way between white walls, I walked aimlessly until I came to a fountain. A slender stream of water dropped from a tap, wounding the smooth surface below without malice. I cupped my hands and drank: the water was cold, refreshing and had a mineral taste. It had come from some place in the mountains to spread its message of relief to the thirsty and then go on to the roots of the olive trees in rows on the hillsides.

As I drank, the face I saw reflected seemed at once strange and familiar. I leaned over the surface of the water and gradually the image took on the features of my grandfather.

"I've made it, Grandpa. I'm in Martos."

The old man looked at me with mischievous eyes and pronounced one of his indisputable maxims:

"No-one should be ashamed of being happy."

Then I realised I was trembling and that my vision was clouding over from the fatigue of the journey. I plunged my face into the fountain, and walked on.

I came to a small square where there was a bar. I went in. The five or six patrons standing at the bar observed me for a few seconds, then went on with their animated conversation.

"What'll it be?" asked the publican.

"I don't know. What do you drink in Martos at this time of day?"

"Wine, *caña* . . . each to his own . . ."

"Give him a dry sherry, Manolo," said one of the patrons.

The publican poured me one, and I tasted it. The same sun that shone outside was in that sherry. I emptied the glass with obvious pleasure.

"Good, isn't it," said the publican.

"Very good."

I wanted to talk with those men, and tell them I had come a long, long way in search of a trace, a shadow, a tiny vestige of my Andalusian roots, but I also wanted to listen to them, to soak up that thick, slightly sullen accent, without the singsong tone you hear down on the coast.

Two new customers came in, two men who had been talking in the street. They ordered two glasses of red wine. One lifted his glass without saying a word, but with a gesture more eloquent than many a speech. The other, more talkative, made a brief speech in reply.

"Good health."

They drank in a sacramental manner. Then, leaving his glass on the bar, the man who had spoken raised the back of his hand to his lips. The world was at peace. Life could not have been more harmonious, so they resumed their conversation.

"So, as I was saying, there could be some money in this tomato business. If it's run properly, of course."

"And the fool, he keeps telling me I've got rheumatism. Rheumatism! Me! Have you ever heard anything so stupid?"

"The Dutch make a fortune out of tomatoes. But tell me, what do they do for sun, the Dutch?"

"And that I should go to some hot baths. What do they reckon we are, playboys or something, these Social Security doctors. Christ Almighty!"

"You can't grow a good tomato in a cage. Have you seen the tomatoes they get in Torredonjimeno? Sun and streamwater, that's what tomatoes need."

"That's what I say: a good plaster, best thing for aching bones; saved a lot of dogs too. Shit! I didn't realise it was so late."

"Off you go, Pepe. Dinner time. Say hello to your relative for me, and maybe we'll get together again some time soon and go on talking. Keep well."

"Well, you know how it is."

"You're telling me, Pepe."

The one who apparently didn't have rheumatism left, and suddenly one of my grandfather's memories of Martos came back to me.

"Is there a Hunter's bar in Martos?"

"Not that I know," said the publican.

"What do you mean there isn't?" interrupted the tomato-grower.

"Well, let's see: there's Miguel's bar, the Castle, the Peña . . ."

"Think, Manolo. What was *this* bar called before?"

"It's had a few names. Let me think."

"Until 1950 it was called the Hunter's bar. Jesus, you're forgetting everything."

"I was only born in 1952. How do you expect me to know that?"

"He's right. It was called the Hunter's bar, and there were two hooks beside the door. One for hanging up knapsacks and the other for shotguns. *I* remember it, anyway," added one of the other patrons.

So, quite possibly, I was in the very place where my grandfather would come to down a few dry sherries.

Once the business about the name of the bar had been sorted out, the men looked at me with unabashed curiosity, so I told them why I was there. I told them about my grandfather and the long journey that had led me to Martos. While I was speaking, some of them telephoned home to say they wouldn't be coming back for lunch, and others sent the same message with some kids who had come in to buy ice creams. The publican, who didn't want to miss a word, simply left the bottles on the bar. When I finished, they looked at one another.

"God, what a story! There's a guy here with the same surname as you. He lives nearby. He's an old-timer, and I think he's called Angel," said the tomato man.

"Yes indeed. He's called Angel and he lives with his wife. But I don't think he's from Martos. I think he's from Segovia," put in a third.

"Come on! Don Angel has lived here ever since I can remember," declared the tomato man.

"Do you know when your grandfather was born?"

"Yes, I know the date."

"What we ought to do is ask the priest. He knows more about what goes on in Martos than anyone."

"Of course. He sticks his nose in everywhere."

"That's his job. The pastrycook has his cakes to tend, and the priest has the old women to gossip with."

"But when he's eating, and he will be now, he's not at home for Jesus Christ himself."

"We can wait. Manolo, what about giving us some *tapas*?"

By four in the afternoon, we had disposed of nearly half a ham and exhausted the supply of tortilla. Newcomers joined the group and were rapidly filled in by those who knew the story already.

Led by the tomato man, we set off to see the priest. But first I tried to pay the bill.

"What are you talking about? Listening to your story was better than watching telly. Hang on, I'm coming to see the priest too," declared the publican.

The priest was at least seventy, the sort who wears a cassock. Looking as if we had given him a scare, he came forward to face the group that had burst into the peace of his church.

"What are you after here?"

"Relax, Father, our intentions are pure."

"The reason I ask is that I never see you at Mass."

The tomato man, already instated as the group's spokesman, told the priest my story and explained the reasons for my visit. The priest then led us into a room with a high ceiling and walls covered with books bound long ago. It didn't take him long to locate my grandfather's baptism certificate.

"Come over here," the priest called to me.

The volume he held had seen more than a century go by. In it were the names of my grandfather and my great-grandparents: Gerardo del Carmen, son of Carlos Ismael and Virginia del Pilar. The document bore witness to the first public act of a man described perfectly by the Peruvian poet César Vallejo's lines: 'He was born a tiny little child looking at the sky, then he grew, turned red, struggled with his cells, his hungers, his bits and pieces, his no's, his even so's . . .', and who, in the course of his life, became well acquainted with prison, persecution and exile, for the sake of his libertarian ideas.

"They're right," said the priest as he accompanied me to the door. "You go up the street of the Virgin to number twelve. That's where Angel lives, your grandfather's younger brother, the only one of the five brothers who is still alive. You'll have to shout, because he's deaf as a post. God bless you for having found him. It's a miracle."

The news of the miracle was travelling fast: some little old ladies made the sign of the Cross as I passed them on the way out of the church. Followed by a good-sized retinue, I went up the street of the Virgin, and stopped in front of number twelve.

The house was white, with a green wooden door. I didn't dare knock, and none of my companions took the initiative. They all remained silent, and looking at those sun-tanned faces, I had the feeling that there was something tragic about the situation, but I couldn't work out why.

Years later, when I found out all I ever would about Martos, I understood that in this region – the most impoverished, though not the poorest, part of Andalusia – sooner or later, the men set off on the road down to the coast, and never came back. And if one of them did come back, he was invariably a failure.

"What's your problem, stickybeaks? Don't you have anything to do?" said the tomato man, and the retinue began to back off.

"Go on, back to business or this sun'll dry up what brains you have left," added another.

"You'll stop by at the bar afterwards, won't you?" said the publican as he turned to go.

They left me alone in front of the door. Before knocking, I felt its rough surface with my hand. The deep green colour it had been painted attracted and retained the warmth of the sun. I left my hand there, hoping that energy would flow into my body and give me the courage to knock. But I didn't need to, because the door gave way to the pressure of my touch.

I pushed, and then I saw the old man.

He was sleeping peacefully, lying back in a beach chair under the shade of a lemon tree. The door opened directly onto a paved patio. Beyond it stood the house, uniformly white, and everywhere there were geraniums in pots. Beside the old man was a table, and on it a glass of water and a few sugar cubes. I looked at the paving stones for a link with my childhood, and there it was, in the form of two or three squashed flies, dried out by the sun.

My grandfather used to play the same game: he would put a bit of sugar in his mouth, moisten it with a mouthful of water, and spit out the mixture. Then he would place one foot just above the sweet trap and wait for the flies to come. Then, squish!

"Oh, Gerardo! How can you be so cruel?" my grandmother would say in reproof.

"It's a service to humanity. If these little beasts evolve they turn into priests or soldiers," replied my grandfather.

I squatted in front of the old man, taking care not to disturb his rest. He was sleeping with his head leaning slightly towards one shoulder. Sometimes his lips and eyebrows moved. I wondered what images inhabited his dreams. Perhaps among them was his brother Gerardo, still a lad, picking olives, or the two of them walking together down the hill towards Jaén to see a bullfight one Sunday, or looking down into the void over the edge of the Rock of Martos, from which the condemned men used to be thrown.

With his face thoroughly furrowed by wrinkles and framed by a sparse white beard, he seemed in good health. His body was thin, and his large hands and thick fingers were those of a farmer. His legs were long, like my grandfather's. Good legs for walking.

Suddenly, he opened his eyes. I saw myself reflected in

his grey pupils, which shone alertly. He was fitting my image into his memories.

"You're Paquito, the milk lady's son."

"No, I'm not Paquito."

"I can't hear you, son. What did you say?"

"No, Don Angel, I'm not Paquito," I said, raising my voice.

"So you're Miguelillo. And about time you came, my boy."

"Don Angel, do you remember your brother Gerardo?"

Then the old man's gaze passed through my skin, examined each one of my bones, went out the door, into the street, up and down hills, visiting every tree, every drop of olive oil, every vine's shade, every obliterated footprint, every round sung, every bull sacrificed at the fateful hour, every sunset, every civil guard who came to the farm as if he had a right, every piece of news that arrived from so far away, every letter that never got sent because, hell, you know how it is, every silence that grew longer and longer until the absoluteness of distance became a certainty.

"Gerardo . . . the one they called the Snake?"

He was slippery, my grandfather. Feared and sought after. He changed skins and names to safeguard his one rebellious love.

"Yes, Don Angel. They used to call him that."

181

"My brother . . . the one who went to America?"

Yes. The one who went to America. One among so many who boarded the ships full of hope. Spaniards who, four centuries after the armed invasion of America, set out in search of peace and were welcomed and found wood to build their houses, the noble wax of industrious bees to polish their tables, dry wines to shape new dreams and a land that said to them: the place you feel best is where you belong.

My grandfather. The one who went to America. Who went over the sea and on the other side found receptive ears waiting for his words: "The social contract is an odious idea dreamed up by the enemies of humanity. The natural way to sort out our troubles is by talking them through in a spirit of brotherhood. You can't impose rules where life's rules are already in force," said my grandfather when I went with him as a boy to the Workers' Solidarity evenings.

"Yes, Don Angel. The one who went to America."

"You're my brother then?"

Deep inside me, my grandfather was urging me to reply: "Yes, say yes and hug him. All men are brothers, and it is in defenceless old age that the fragile, eternal truths come to the surface."

"No, Don Angel, your brother Gerardo was my grandfather."

A serious look came into the old man's countenance. He sat back in the chair, put his sinewy hands on his knees and examined me from head to foot, from shoulder to shoulder. Did he want to see a certificate? Maybe he wanted me to open my chest and show him my heart?

"María," he called.

An old woman in deep mourning came out of the house. Her silver hair was tied up in a bun and she stood watching me with a kind expression. Then Don Angel cleared his throat and pronounced the most beautiful poem life has rewarded me with, and I knew that at last I had come full circle: I was at the starting point of the journey my grandfather began. Don Angel said:

"María, bring some wine, a relative has come from America."

Notes on these Notes

IN THE house of Mari Carmen and Paco Ignacio Taibo I in Mexico there is a huge table around which twenty-four dinner guests may gather. Sitting there once I heard a phrase which serves as the title of one of Taibo's books: 'Against the current of forgetting'. When I read the book later, my affection and admiration for the Asturian writer grew, and at the same time I realised that it is impossible to avoid parting with certain texts, no matter how attached to them one is and how much they seem a fundamental part of one's private life.

I have finally parted with these notes, which have come a long way with me and were always there to remind me that I have practically no right to feel alone or depressed, or to fly the flag at half-mast.

187

They were written in various places and situations. I never knew what to call them, and I still don't.

Somebody once said to me that I must have lots of things in the bottom of my drawers, and since the assertion surprised me, I asked him to tell me what he meant.

"The bottom of the drawer is where you keep the notes you make without knowing why or what for," he explained.

No. These are not bottom-of-the-drawer texts, because that would presuppose the existence of a drawer, which is normally part of a desk, and I don't have a desk. Nor do I want one, since I write on a thick board inherited from an old baker in Hamburg.

One afternoon while playing *skatt*, a card game peculiar to northern Germany, the old baker announced to his companions that because of his arthritis he was going to have to throw in the towel and shut down the bakery.

"So what are you going to do now, you stingy old bastard?" asked one of the affable card players.

"Well, since none of my sons want to take over the business and my machines have been declared obsolete, I'll just chuck it all out and give away the things that have some sentimental value," replied old Jan Keller, before inviting us to a long party in the bakery.

That's how I came into possession of the thick board on which he kneaded bread dough for fifty years, and on which

I knead my stories now. I love this board, which smells of the noblest of professions, of yeast, sesame and ginger. So, really, what use is a desk to me?

These notes, which I can't think what to call, lay about on a shelf somewhere gathering dust. From time to time, looking for old photos or documents, I would come across them, and I confess that I read them with a mixture of tenderness and pride, because in those scribbled or clumsily typed pages I had made an attempt to come to terms with two themes of capital importance, aptly defined by the Argentinian writer Julio Cortázar: understanding what it means to be human, and understanding what it means to be an artist.

It is true that there is much personal experience here, but this should not be interpreted as a way of keeping Alzheimer's disease at bay, and I can assure you I am not planning to write my memoirs.

Some of these notes came out of their hiding places over the years to be published in anthologies, journals and in a condensed edition in Italy.

They have finally taken the form of the book you are now holding, thanks to the wise and loyal guidance of Beatriz de Moura. I called this book *Patagonia Express**
in homage to the train, which, although it no longer exists, poetry having proven unprofitable in recent years, goes on

travelling in the memories of the men and women of Patagonia.

You have accompanied me on a journey without a fixed itinerary, along with all the wonderful people who have appeared here under their real names, from whom I have learnt and go on learning so much.

Lanzarote, Canary Islands
August 1995

---

* *The title of the original Spanish edition (Barcelona: Tusquets Editores, 1995).*

Glossary

boleadoras: hunting weapon used by Patagonian Indians, consisting of several round stones joined by a leather strap

cabrales: soft, strong-tasting cheese made from cow, sheep and goat's milk

caña: distilled liquor made from sugar cane

chata: sturdy truck

chimichurri: spicy marinade often served with roast or grilled meat

chiripá: skirt-like garment hitched up in front between the legs, worn by gauchos

Confederación Nacional del Trabajo (CNT): Spanish anarchist trade union

empanada: pastry turnover containing vegetables, hard-boiled egg, olives, beef, chicken, ham or cheese

fabada: Asturian stew made of beans, pork sausage and bacon

gaucho: skilled horseman of the pampa

How the Steel was Tempered: Nikolay Ostrovsky's (1904-36) autobiographical novel is regarded as one of the classics of Socialist Realism; it was originally translated as *The Making of a Hero*

maté: South American tea-like beverage brewed from the dried, chopped leaf of *Ilex paraguariensis*, the preparation and consumption of which is a cultural practice which transcends ethnicity, class and occupation. The tea is shared from gourds, which range from simple wooden vessels to elaborate silver museum pieces.

Open Veins of Latin America: Five Centuries of the Pillage of a Continent: highly influential anticolonialist history by the Uruguayan writer Eduardo Galeano (1940-), first published in 1971

tapas: snacks served in Spanish bars
truco: card game played in South America's southern regions; play is accompanied by rhyming verse, and partner communication through facial signals is allowed

LONELY PLANET JOURNEYS

JOURNEYS is a unique collection of travellers' tales – published by the company that understands travel better than anyone else.

It is a series for anyone who has ever experienced – or dreamed of – the magical moment when they encountered a strange culture or saw a place for the first time. They are tales to read while you're planning a trip, while you're on the road or while you're in an armchair, in front of a fire.

Lonely Planet guidebooks have always gone beyond providing simple nuts-and-bolts information, so it is a short step to JOURNEYS, a new series of outstanding titles that will explore our planet through the eyes of a fascinating and diverse group of international travellers.

JOURNEYS books will catch the spirit of a place, illuminate a culture, recount a crazy adventure, or introduce a fascinating way of life. They will always entertain, and always enrich the experience of travel.

THE GATES OF DAMASCUS
Lieve Joris
Translated by Sam Garrett

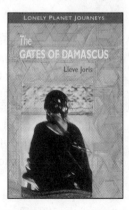

This best-selling book is a beautifully drawn portrait of day-to-day life in modern Syria. Through her intimate contact with local people, Lieve Joris draws us into the fascinating world that lies behind the gates of Damascus. Hala's husband is a political prisoner, jailed for his opposition to the Assad regime; through the author's friendship with Hala we see how Syrian politics impacts on the lives of ordinary people.

Written after the Gulf War, *The Gates of Damascus* offers a unique insight into the complexities of the Arab world.

ISLANDS IN THE CLOUDS
Travels in the Highlands of New Guinea
Isabella Tree

This is the fascinating account of a journey to the remote and beautiful Highlands of Papua New Guinea and Irian Jaya: one of the most extraordinary and dangerous regions on the planet. The author travels with a PNG Highlander who introduces her to his intriguing and complex world, which is changing rapidly as it collides with twentieth-century technology and the island's developing social and political systems. *Islands in the Clouds* is a thoughtful, moving book, full of insights into a region that is rarely noticed by the rest of the world.

LOST JAPAN
Alex Kerr

Lost Japan draws on the author's personal experiences of Japan over thirty years. Alex Kerr takes his readers on a backstage tour, exploring different facets of his involvement with the country: friendships with Kabuki actors, buying and selling art, studying calligraphy, exploring rarely visited temples and shrines . . .

The Japanese edition of this book was awarded the 1994 Shincho Gakugei Literature Prize for the best work of non-fiction: the first time a foreigner has won this prestigious award.

SEAN & DAVID'S LONG DRIVE

Sean Condon

Sean and David are young townies who have rarely strayed beyond city limits. One day, for no good reason, they set out to discover their homeland, and what follows is a wildly entertaining adventure that covers half of Australia. Highlights include the weekly Hair Wax Report and a Croc-Spotting with Stew adventure.

Sean Condon has written a hilarious, offbeat road book that mixes sharp insights with deadpan humour and outright lies.

SHOPPING FOR BUDDHAS

Jeff Greenwald

'Here in this distant, exotic land, we were compelled to raise the art of shopping to an experience that was, on the one hand, almost Zen – and, on the other hand, tinged with desperation like shopping at Macy's or Bloomingdale's during a one-day-only White Sale.'

Shopping for Buddhas is Jeff Greenwald's story of his obsessive search for the perfect Buddha statue. In the backstreets of Kathmandu, he discovers more than he bargained for . . . and his souvenir-hunting turns into an ironic metaphor for the clash between spiritual riches and material greed. Politics, religion and serious shopping collide in this witty account of an enlightening visit to Nepal.

RELATED TITLES
FROM LONELY PLANET

South America on a shoestring
This practical guide provides concise information for budget travellers and covers South America from the Darien Gap to Tierra del Fuego.

Chile & Easter Island – travel survival kit
Travel in Chile is easy, with possibilities as varied as the countryside. This guide also gives detailed coverage of Chile's Pacific outpost, the mysterious Easter Island.

Ecuador & the Galápagos Islands – travel survival kit
Ecuador offers a wide variety of travel experiences, from the high cordilleras to the Amazon plains – and 600 miles west, the fascinating Galápagos islands. Everything you need to know about travelling around this enchanting country.

Trekking in the Patagonian Andes
The first detailed guide to this region gives information on 28 walks, and lists a number of other possibilities extending from the Araucanía and Lake District regions of Argentina and Chile to the remote icy of South America and Tierra del Fuego.

Latin American Spanish phrasebook
From Texas to Patagonia – you'll never be stuck for words. This practical phrasebook covers all the essential words and phrases you'll need to get by on your travels.

Quechua phrasebook
Quechua (Runasimi) is the ancient 'mouth of the People' of the Incan Empire. It is still spoken in parts of Chile and Ecuador, and a little knowledge of it will help travellers communicate effectively.

Chile travel atlas
Make your journey to Chile with the handiest and most accurate maps available – the Lonely Planet travel atlas to Chile. This atlas covers all national parks and the comprehensive index ensures easy location-finding. A detailed legend and travel information in five languages is also included.

PLANET TALK

Lonely Planet's FREE quarterly newsletter

Every issue of PLANET TALK is packed with up-to-date travel news and advice including:

- a letter from Lonely Planet founders Tony and Maureen Wheeler
- travel diary from a Lonely Planet author – find out what it's really like out on the road
- feature article on an important and topical travel issue
- a selection of recent letters from our readers
- the latest travel news from all over the world
- details on Lonely Planet's new and forthcoming releases

To join our mailing list contact any Lonely Planet office.

LONELY PLANET PUBLICATIONS

Australia: PO Box 617, Hawthorn 3122, Victoria
tel: (03) 9819 1877 fax: (03) 9819 6459
e-mail: talk2us@lonelyplanet.com.au

USA: Embarcadero West, 155 Filbert St, Suite 251,
Oakland, CA 94607
tel: (510) 893 8555 TOLL FREE: 800 275-8555
fax: (510) 893 8563   e-mail: info@lonelyplanet.com

UK: 10 Barley Mow Passage, Chiswick, London W4 4PH
tel: (0181) 742 3161 fax: (0181) 742 2772
e-mail: 100413.3551@compuserve.com

France: 71 bis rue du Cardinal Lemoine, 75005 Paris
tel: 1 44 32 06 20 fax: 1 46 34 72 55
e-mail: 100560.415@compuserve.com

World Wide Web: Lonely Planet is now accesible via the World Wide Web. For travel information and an up-to-date catalogue, you can find us at http://www.lonelyplanet.com/

THE LONELY PLANET STORY

Lonely Planet published its first book in 1973 in response to the numerous 'How did you do it?' questions Maureen and Tony Wheeler were asked after driving, bussing, hitching, sailing and railing their way from England to Australia.

Written at a kitchen table and hand collated, trimmed and stapled, *Across Asia on the Cheap* became an instant local bestseller, inspiring thoughts of another book.

Eighteen months in South-East Asia resulted in their second guide, *South-East Asia on a shoestring*, which they put together in a backstreet Chinese hotel in Singapore in 1975. The 'yellow bible' as it quickly became known to backpackers around the world, soon became *the* guide to the region. It has sold well over half a million copies and is now in its 8th edition, still retaining its familiar yellow cover.

Today there are over 180 titles, including travel guides, walking guides, language kits & phrasebooks, travel atlases and travel literature. The company is one of the largest travel publishers in the world. Although Lonely Planet initially specialised in guides to Asia, we now cover most regions of the world, including the Pacific, North America, South America, Africa, the Middle East and Europe.

The emphasis continues to be on travel for independent travellers. Tony and Maureen still travel for several months of each year and play an active part in the writing, updating and quality control of Lonely Planet's guides.

They have been joined by over 70 authors and 170 staff at our offices in Melbourne (Australia), Oakland (USA), London (UK) and Paris (France). Travellers themselves also make a valuable contribution to the guides through the feedback we receive in thousands of letters each year.

The people at Lonely Planet strongly believe that travellers can make a positive contribution to the countries they visit, both through their appreciation of the countries' culture, wildlife and natural features, and through the money they spend. In addition, the company makes a direct contribution to the countries and regions it covers. Since 1986 a percentage of the income from each book has been donated to ventures such as famine relief in Africa; aid projects in India; agricultural projects in Central America; Greenpeace's efforts to halt French nuclear testing in the Pacific; and Amnesty International.

'I hope we send the people out with the right attitude about travel. You realise when you travel that there are so many different perspectives about the world, so we hope these books will make people more interested in what they see.'

                                                                    – Tony Wheeler